WHAT PEOPLE A

SEEING THE GOOD IN
UNFAMILIAR SPIRITUALITIES

This book touches a raw nerve. Like the authors of Godless Morality and God: A Guide for the Perplexed, it takes seriously the religious and moral sentiments of an age which has largely given up on organized religion but which is eager to know and feel the Divine purpose and destiny of all humanity. It is a morally serious book critically engaging with a wide range of spiritual quests, treasuring what is authentic and eschewing what is trivial and even dangerous. The author's creative mind and poetic style provide the reader with a unique moral compass by which to explore the contemporary spiritual landscape. Inspired by the writings of the Hebrew prophet Ezekiel, this book promises to become a spiritual classic in our time and deserves to be widely read.
Myra N Blyth, Chaplain; Tutorial Fellow in Worship and Pastoral Studies, Regent's Park College, Oxford University

This important little book dares to address some of the most pressing issues of our time: human rights, the conflict between atheism and religion, suffering, the challenges of pluralism, beliefs about the afterlife and human destiny. It does so without tired dogmas but with powerful images that release one's imagination. I hope that Gethin Abraham-Williams receives a wide hearing; humanity will be better for it.
Gregory A. Barker, Senior Lecturer in Religious Studies, The University of Wales: Trinity Saint David and editor of *Jesus in the World's Faiths* and, with Stephen E. Gregg, *Jesus Beyond Christianity: The Classic Texts*

The life of the Spirit flows through the metaphorical rivers of the Jordan and the Tigris, and in between we encounter the liminal prophet, Ezekiel, who holds the tension of creative transformation – as the old fades and a new stage in the religious imagination awaits its hour. Gethin Abraham-Williams explores this age-old spiritual dynamic, seeking to illuminate the shifting nature of spirituality in our time. The ensuing synthesis is rich in insight, wisdom and hope. A treasured resource as we journey through today's changing spiritual landscape.

Diarmuid O'Murchu MSC, Social Psychologist and author of *Ancestral Grace*

An intriguing account, rooted in the author's biblical knowledge and drawing on his rich experience as a practitioner. This book has much to recommend it, offering a spirituality that 'spans our religious past and makes sense of our uncertain future'.

Lavinia Byrne, religious commentator and author

In an increasingly plural world, it is vital for Christians, people of other faith and people of no religion but 'good faith' to get beyond the stereotypes that often characterise debates about religion and secularity. Gethin Abraham-Williams encourages us to do just that, and offers a stimulating and necessarily provocative interpretation of what is happening in a mixed-belief society and how we might respond.

Simon Barrow, Co-director of Ekklesia, the religion and society think-tank

Seeing the Good in

UNFAMILIAR SPIRITUALITIES

Reacting against the relentless secularism of life in the West today, many are turning to alternative spiritualities for meaning and direction. Rejecting the familiar, but seemingly untenable beliefs they grew up with, many are open to new ways of believing; to new ways of living responsible, spiritually sensitive lives. This book is about engaging with the spiritually unfamiliar without feeling threatened by it.

Seeing the Good in

UNFAMILIAR SPIRITUALITIES

Reacting against the relentless secularism of life in the West today, many are turning to alternative spiritualities for meaning and direction. Rejecting the familiar, but seemingly untenable beliefs they grew up with, many are open to new ways of believing; to new ways of living responsible, spiritually sensitive lives. This book is about engaging with the spiritually unfamiliar without feeling threatened by it.

Gethin Abraham-Williams

Winchester, UK
Washington, USA

First published by Circle Books, 2011
Circle Books is an imprint of John Hunt Publishing Ltd., Laurel House, Station Approach,
Alresford, Hants, SO24 9JH, UK
office1@o-books.net
www.o-books.com

For distributor details and how to order please visit the 'Ordering' section on our website.

Text copyright: Gethin Abraham-Williams 2010

ISBN: 978 1 84694 499 4

A CIP catalogue record for this book is available from the British Library.

Design: Stuart Davies

Printed in the UK by CPI Antony Rowe
Printed in the USA by Offset Paperback Mfrs, Inc

We operate a distinctive and ethical publishing philosophy in all
areas of our business, from our global network of authors to
production and worldwide distribution.

CONTENTS

GETHIN ABRAHAM-WILLIAMS, an Oxford University graduate in Theology, is a Baptist minister, and a Cardiff University tutor in the Bible in the Contemporary World. He's a member of the British and Irish Living Spirituality Network, and of various ecumenical and inter-faith groups, for which he was awarded the Cross of St Augustine by the Archbishop of Canterbury in 2006.

For our son and daughter
Owain and Ellen

asking the right questions and engaging with today's answers

Preface

'Eastern spirituality, Paganism, Spiritualism, Theosophy, alternative science and medicine, popular psychology' and 'a range of beliefs emanating out of a general interest in the paranormal' are the marks of today's 'new spiritual awakening'. Such is the conclusion drawn by Christopher Partridge at the end of his monumental book, *The Re-Enchantment of the West*.

Add the presence and practice of sizeable numbers of people pursuing some of the other great religions of the world, not on the other side of the world but on our own doorstep, coupled with a scientific revolution quietly broadening our perspectives, and it is not surprising if many feel disoriented and confused.

It is, however, not the first time we have had to face the prospect of a spiritual re-alignment on such a seismic scale. Something similar was going on in the Axial period (between 800 and 200 BCE), when concepts of God, from India to Greece, from China to the Fertile Crescent, were undergoing huge and radical changes.

One of those caught up in this ferment of ideas was the young Hebrew guru, Ezekiel. Trapped between the river Jordan's traditional, but inadequate, theology and the enticing spiritualities of the river Tigris' glittering Babylonian empire, Ezekiel had the insight and the courage to reshape his people's beliefs in a way that not only served their needs at the time, but bequeathed a challenge to the world ever since.

Fragments of Ezekiel's highly unconventional career and pronouncements have come down to us in the book that now bears his name among the prophets of the Hebrew canon. We do not have to agree with all of his conclusions to recognize in this remarkable man's life, hints and whispers of a spirituality that moderates between the old and the new, and whose spirituality is still shot through with intensity and hope.

This book is addressed to those who feel themselves to be similarly stranded between two worlds: the familiar, but seemingly untenable one they grew up with, and the unfamiliar, but possibly more responsible one, where they can rediscover God as both credible and attractive. This book is about the rediscovery of a God who is depicted in one of the oldest creation stories, as 'walking about in the garden at the time of the evening breeze', when shadows soften and the colors mix.

It is addressed primarily to those who are reluctant to give up on a God who, they believe, is most often revealed in the twilight of sundown, rather than in the glare of noonday.

Foreword

I happened to be reading the manuscript for this book during the week that Professor Stephen Hawking declared categorically that God did not create the universe. In Hawking's view, modern physics leaves no place for a creator. Although not every scientist would agree with Professor Hawking, this book, nevertheless, highlights the problems that many people of faith face; they no longer believe in God in the same way as their ancestors did because of the findings of modern science and yet they want to hang on to a belief in a transcendent being.

This book shows how these two seemingly contradictory things can be reconciled and how it is possible to believe in God without abandoning either the insights of modern scientific discoveries or recent biblical scholarship. It does so by showing how the prophet Ezekiel carried on believing in God during the crisis he and the Jewish nation went through when most of the population was captured by the Babylonians and carried off into exile, and so felt totally abandoned by God.

Using a wide variety of sources, the author shows how having faith is not always as comfortable an exercise as organized religion tries to make it. He argues that true faith is being able to face all the problems which believing in God entail, a God who is present with us whatever happens, for nothing is beyond his redemptive love. Faith that is tested can become stronger, as the Book of Job illustrates.

Gethin Abraham-Williams writes poetically, perceptively and simply about complicated and difficult matters. It is a book that could help many who want an intelligent and creative faith.

The Most Rev Dr Barry Morgan, Archbishop of Wales

This is an in-between land; a land without clear borders, with misty, uncertain edges; a land of infinite possibility. It's a land of story and strange tales: tales of seas parting to allow escapes from slavery, of burning bushes not burnt, of water turning into wine, of glorious visions on mountain tops ... It's a land conjured in the hidden-ness of poetry, in the nuances of music, the magnificence of great vistas, the fragility of beauty and friendship.
Bridget Hewitt

Prophesy to the wind, prophesy, man, and say to it, 'These are the words of the Lord God: Come, O wind, come from every quarter and breathe into these slain, that they may come to life.' I began to prophesy as he had bidden me: breath came into them; they came to life and rose to their feet, a mighty host.
Ezekiel

Popular interpretation tends to dismiss Ezechiel as 'bizarre'. But Ezechiel may be exactly the right text for such a 'bizarre' time as ours.
Walter Brueggemann

I am caught between a church that once assumed a kingly role and a church that now awaits an uncertain future.
Stanley Hauerwas

1. Making for the Middle Ground

To be, or not to be, that is the question
Shakespeare: *Hamlet* (III, i, 55)

It is Sunday morning, and the sheltered, sheltering town between the Ystwyth and the Rheidol rivers is not yet wide awake. Students of law, agriculture and international politics turn over in their university sleep, and holidaymakers search the uncertain horizon for signs of the sun. In the bay, deep below the waves, only the dolphins enquiringly hear the muffled peal of a lost Atlantis, *Cantre'r Gwaelod*. Beyond the pebbly beach and the concrete breakers, the crumbling cliffs and the prim promenade, other bells soon rouse some to pray, and some to sing, and some to test another sermon. Not as many as once. Not anymore. But not so few either.

And in the town's church-peppered, chapel-salted streets, many will still turn out and turn up to celebrate the certainties of faith; or to face, or face down, its uncertainties. Some to find their doubts anaesthetized by notes from organ and choir and time-worn liturgies; others to take their battered heads and bruised souls back into the ring for more bouts with words, ancient and modern, enunciated and garbled, from pulpit, altar and lectern, only to limp out an hour later defeated, but unwilling to retire. Cultural believers, harboring a hole where their predecessors caressed a Christ; envious of anyone who could begin a Christmas poem,

And is it true? And is it true,
this most tremendous tale of all?

but more, to end it with the certainty,

That God was Man in Palestine

And lives today in Bread and Wine.

Springtime Hill

But our story starts further back, much further back, and farther away, in a place that is also between two rivers, the Jordan and the Tigris. The Jordan watered the land that the Hebrews inhabited, and the Tigris spawned the mighty Mesopotamian Empire of Babylon that held sway over most of that part of the world in the sixth century BCE.

In the year 597, those two rivers were destined to become symbols for a development of ideas with far reaching consequences for the world ever since. In that year, a large contingent of Hebrews was forcibly removed from the banks of the Jordan to be resettled by their Babylonian conquerors on the banks of the Tigris, at Tel-abib, Springtime Hill, and the Keber canal. It was an exile that traumatized the Hebrews, but that also gave birth to some of the most original spiritual thinkers to have come from that part of the world. Among them, Ezekiel: an odd genius.

Babylon, the center of the Chaldean hegemony, has come down to us in the Biblical record as the epitome of a debauched and cruel place, carried over into Christian writings as a code name for an equally oppressive, successive world power: Rome. But Babylon must have been an eye-opener for the God-fearing exiles from provincial Jerusalem.

The city itself was utterly magnificent. Here was wealth beyond their imagining and architecture on a grand scale. Here they would be made to question whether the Mosaic Decalogue itself may have been a derivative of the legal code of Babylon's first king, Hammurabi. Here were philosophers and artists, thinkers and craftsmen, performers and entertainers in abundance. The place was spectacularly cosmopolitan, teeming with life and color.

This hub of the then-known world bombarded their restricted experience with ideas and images that were as exciting as they were disturbing. The scale and the sophistication of it intrigued as much as it unsettled them. Medicine, chemistry and alchemy rubbed shoulders with botany, zoology and astronomy in its souks; the Babylonian numbering system was more advanced than anything in the then-known world. What were the ideas that sustained this people and had allowed them to attain such a dominant position among the nations?

It was in this maelstrom of meanings that the exiled priest, Ezekiel, molded his thinking and started entertaining God-thoughts that seemed frighteningly novel, but that would eventually become the core of a renewed spirituality. He, of course, was not to know that, when the awesome power of the Chaldean Army broke through his settled world, its swords flaying, its arrows flying, its cavalry terrifying, to march him and many of his compatriots six hundred miles eastwards, away from Jerusalem, away from the Jordan, across the desert wastes; the distance, conceptually as well as geographically, unbearable.

Humiliated and mocked, paraded as the human spoil of conquest, they were led behind their vanquished king through the streets of Babylon, to be gawped at and gloried over by a populace hungry for the spectacle of triumph.

The young king of Judah, Jehoiachin, had barely three months to settle into the role after the sudden death of his father. But the old king had backed the wrong horse. The alliance with Egypt had come to nothing, and Nebuchadnezzar had decided to swat the fly that was Judah. He left enough of the old guard behind to maintain the basic functions of the country, but from then on it was to be no more than a Babylonian province.

For Ezekiel and some of his fellow priests, life on Babylon's Springtime Hill may have been relatively easy. They were among the more fortunate ones, part of the elite of Hebrew society expected to keep company with their deposed King and his court. The rest, the hewers of wood and the fetchers of water, were put to work maintaining the enemy's economy, many of them slaving away to complete the Keber canal, one of King Nebuchadnezzar's key domestic projects. Others were in fear that their sons might fall for foreign women, their daughters be coveted and courted by foreign men.

They were, nevertheless, allowed their day of rest to say their prayers, sing their psalms, make their sacrifices, maintain their customs, but all the time this hankering after Jerusalem, Zion, the seat of the Most High, the guardian of Israel. Only this time he hadn't protected them; and they couldn't understand why.

What were the legendary Hanging Gardens compared with the wild and wonderful hills of Judah, the lemons and oranges of its citrus groves? Was not Jordan the entrance to their promised land? What was Nebuchadnezzar's 'ziggurat', his stepped tower, his Babel, but a plinth for the idol, Marduk, compared with the Holy of Holies of their Jewish God in the temple Solomon had built? Were not the gates of Jerusalem, through which King David had danced when he brought home the Ark of the Covenant, more precious to God than those that guarded the entrance to this strange and alien place, with its foreign ways and its difficult, guttural tongue?

Over the years, the images and impressions multiplied and proliferated, never getting any easier to assimilate, absorb, process and categorize, until the day Ezekiel crossed an invisible line in his thinking and his praying, and began to feel his way to the uncertain possibility of a new theology, of a new understanding of the Numinous One they'd known and worshipped in the temple back in Jerusalem.

Putting aside the undeniable oddity of some of Ezekiel behavior, the account of his life and his utterances reveal a substantial figure with the moral courage and the inner compunction to grapple with ideas of God and of human existence in a highly creative way, His legacy contributed to the survival of his people by enabling them to redefine their beliefs in a way that restored their theological self-confidence. It also provided a model for successive generations in widely disparate cultures to cope with change by redefining the nature of the relationship between humankind and God.

A Religious Past

In some respects, Ezekiel bears an uncanny similarity to Shakespeare's Hamlet, described by one scholar of the Bard as, 'Poised between a religious past and a secular future'. In Ezekiel's case, however, it seemed as if the religious past was all there was; a past centered almost solely on the Temple in Jerusalem: that special place between earth and heaven where the Hebrews had done business with their particular God, to become his particular people.

Ezekiel had been born and bred in Jerusalem. Buzi, his father, was a respected Temple priest; the family traced their lineage back to the High Priest, Zadok, when David was king. In such a theocracy, the priesthood is always supreme: the spiritual custodians and conscience of the nation as well as the final arbiters of the divine commandments. That was Ezekiel's background; that was his destiny.

Watching his father offering the sacrifices, tending the lamps, chanting the psalms, wafting the incense, reading from the scrolls, Ezekiel had imbibed the faith as earnestly as he'd once sucked his mother's milk. Sometimes he'd seen the lonely figure of old Jeremiah striding through the temple's outer courtyard, and listened to his dreary lamentations and gloomy predictions. But it hadn't challenged him.

Buzi had told the boy not to worry about Jeremiah. What mattered was the Temple and its rituals. That was where he, and indeed all of them, would find the throne of God: mysterious, elusive but always faithful, behind the great curtain in the inner court.

'Have you ever seen God?' the bright eyed, intelligent, wildly imaginative child had remembered once asking his father.

'No, son,' Buzi had answered. 'Only the High Priest goes behind that curtain, and then only once a year at the time of the Great Festival of the Atonement.'

'Did the High Priest tell you what God looked like?' the boy had persisted.

'Son, no one can see the Holy One, the "I will be Who I will be". Even Moses, who gave us the law, who led us out of Egypt, only caught sight of God's shadow. It is enough that we know God is among us.'

Ezekiel had believed his father, but he had also not disbelieved the unpopular prophet who'd haunted the Temple precinct telling them to mend their ways, warning that otherwise there would be an end to their rituals, a cessation to their unique existence. Jeremiah attested he'd been chosen by God before he'd been formed in the womb, consecrated before he'd been born. How could he be so sure, the growing boy pondered? How did he know?

On the banks of the Tigris one hot July day in 593 BCE, all that seemed a lifetime away to the man pacing restlessly in preparation for the delivery of the first of his messages from God. In his mid-thirties, married by now and most likely with children, we can imagine a figure of middling height, perhaps of spare build, taut, austere but impressive, with dark penetrating eyes that could twinkle when he smiled; his thick ebony hair neater than his demeanor suggested; his beard already flecked with stabs of grey.

A sensitive man, Ezekiel's social interaction could, nevertheless, be quite acerbic, even off-putting, as he reacted sharply to a perceived or actual failure by those who should know better. It mattered more to their special and particular God, how they lived than whether they observed religious rites.

He was that strange anomaly: a Temple priest without a Temple; respected, but often misunderstood; his burden to be a prophet to a rootless, landless people. And always the question:

> Will such a vine flourish?
> Will not its roots be torn up
> and its fruit stripped off,
> and all of its freshly sprouted leaves wither,
> until it is uprooted and carried away
> with little effort and a small force?

How was his God, the eternal, faithful, particular God of Abraham and Sarah, of Isaac and Rebecca, of Jacob and Rachel, to be worshipped among this abhorrent pantheon of gods and goddesses: Apsu and Tiamat, Lahmu and Lahamu, Anshar and Kishar? His people had lost their land. Had they also lost their God? The psalmist's agonized prayer was his too:

> My God, by day I cry to you, but there is no answer;
> in the night I cry with no respite.

Could their God be found anywhere, or had they now to suffer that worse exile, of separation, not only from the soil that was forever associated with the God who had moved on the face of the waters and fashioned Adam from its precious clay, but also from the wellspring of their identity and their destiny as God's chosen people?

> Do not remain far from me,
> for trouble is near and I have no helper.

Such questions herald wake-up moments. Because of some trauma, or a shaking of the foundations, they offer us the opportunity to cross from the safe and familiar to the unknown and unpredictable. It is a process that allows us to discover that the reorientation of our belief systems does not also require us to jettison or discard the core of our relationship with the Holy Other, only to see it differently.

It is the Nazi martyr, Dietrich Bonhoeffer's 'coming of age'. It is the American theologian, Paul Tillich's 'courage to be'. It is the space 'between water and water' that stops the extremes from engulfing us, that opens our eyes to a new reality; to a more responsible, a richer way of being. It is eating the apple; it is becoming aware, becoming responsible. It is a crossing of the line; a demarcation that might once have kept us safe, but that ultimately fails to satisfy an enquiring mind or a restless soul.

Ezekiel defied the current consensus that every nation had its particular god, whose sovereignty was limited to a particular patch of earth, pronouncing it unsustainable. Either God was everywhere, or God was nowhere. We have different issues to contend with: militant atheism, the challenge of other faiths, popular fascination with the occult, forgiveness as a philosophy to live by, a lost capacity to admit to our own vulnerability, and how to reclaim the space that lies between me and myself. It will be our capacity to reconfigure our understanding of God in the face of these challenges that are new to us, that will decide whether the God we end up believing in, or not believing in, is a product of our unthinking past, or 'something/someone' much more exciting and dynamic.

*

It was Lesslie Newbigin, a bishop in the Church of South India and an eminent student of the nature and theology of Christian mission, who realized the significance of in-between space for the coming millennium. He enlarged upon it in his book, *The other side of 1984*; a deliberate allusion to George Orwell's satirical novel of post-war totalitarianism and one man's hopeless struggle against it: *Nineteen Eighty-Four*.

Thirty-five years after Orwell wrote his book, Newbigin, who'd spent a lifetime wrestling with the problem of relating faith to public issues, saw a threat to contemporary culture different from that of Orwell. For him, the crisis of Western civilization now was not so much totalitarian, but spiritual; in particular the vacuum created by the post-enlightenment scientific method, which rejects faith as a premise for understanding life. Newbigin argues:

We are at a point in the history of the 'modern' world at which the accepted [i.e. the Enlightenment's scientific method] has become inadequate and a new framework is called for.

For him, this new framework was a much more upfront presentation of Christian Good News, with a specific challenge to the churches of Britain to become increasingly proactive in the public square in promoting a faith-based approach to contemporary life.

At the time, his plea struck a chord with many influential figures inside and outside the churches; twenty thousand copies of *The other side of 1984* were sold, and its author was invited to deliver the Gore lecture in Westminster Abbey and the Warfield lectures at Princeton Theological Seminary in the United States.

There was a high degree of excitement that religion might be on the verge of something new, taking the theory of knowledge, science and history, economics and health, the media and the arts, seriously, with ideas tossed to and fro in an explosion of intellectual enquiry. With knowledge fragmented by so much specialization, it was Newbigin's hope that an attempt to get a picture of the whole, however superficial, was bound to be beneficial.

Maybe it failed to catch on in the way Newbigin intended because it offered no satisfactory rationale in a post-Enlightenment age. In all fairness, however, he'd never argued for a quick-fix solution, claiming not to expect results until 'after about a hundred and fifty years'! Newbigin had also been at pains to affirm that he was not arguing for a return to a pre-Enlightenment Eden, but it was never clear how he proposed to marry a new, faith-based foundation with the obvious benefits that had come from the Enlightenment.

It was also vulnerable to the charge of appearing exclusively Christian. As a challenge specifically to the Christian churches of Britain, a country which was already becoming increasingly multi-cultural, and consequently multi-faith, it offered little encouragement to those wanting to pursue its aims with those of other faiths. For all the differences of specific beliefs, many in those faiths shared the same concern for a rediscovery of an ethical framework for the ordering of society based on shared spiritual values.

The bishop's thesis relied on the premise that 'The (Christian) Gospel is true'. It was a bold claim, and perhaps in the end, an impossible one to justify, because, is it not possible to speak of other world faiths as also 'true', in the sense of revealing insights into the nature of God and of all that exists? Is it not better, as the British astrophysicist and Quaker, Dame Jocelyn Bell, suggests, that 'a search for understanding' is a more attainable goal? Claims to have the 'Truth', so often lead to absolutist positions, which, apart from feeding extremism, ultimately prove unsustainable in the light of fresh understanding, and 'Christian people above all,' the late Archbishop Robert Runcie once said, 'should know that the Truth is not the same as erasing ambiguity'.

Unwilling to forfeit the benefits of the Enlightenment, many are still looking for a different framework for engaging with their culture and their times. Various expressions of contemporary spirituality are, therefore, a response to a restlessness at the heart of humankind which is dissatisfied with the scientific method as the sole explanation of 'how things are'.

For Newbigin, the dilemma had come at the very beginning of his calling as a newly arrived missionary in India, a country in which he was to spend almost the next forty years. He'd been involved in a serious bus accident that laid him off work for two years. 'How to "explain" it?' he asked himself.

'The Indian pastor said: "It is the will of God." A Hindu would have said: "The karma of your former lives has caught up with you." In some cultures the explanation would be that an enemy had put a curse on me,' Newbigin reflected; adding that if, as an 'enlightened' European, he 'had said that it was because the brakes were not working properly that would have been, for others, no explanation at all. It would have been simply a re-statement of what had to be explained.'

Newbigin's thesis, and the debate it initiated, was an attempt to provide an explanation, because, as he affirmed, 'To speak of an "explanation" is to speak of the ultimate framework of axioms and assumptions by means of which one "makes sense of things".' His 'explanation', however, wasn't convincing enough because the search for understanding is always better than an 'unembarrassed offering of the Christian "dogma"', which had been Newbigin's aim.

Story and Meaning

On the banks of the Tigris, as he looked at the gathering crowd, Ezekiel produced a scroll from under the folds in his tunic, and unrolled it. It was quite unlike any of the ones they'd brought with them from the Temple in Jerusalem. Those had been beautiful creations, protected in highly embroidered sleeves, the Hebrew characters neatly and carefully inscribed on the very best parchment, not to be tampered with; scrolls recalling the stories of their past; stories pregnant with meaning; epics of Creation; the sagas of their founding fathers; proverbs and Psalms; tales about their kings; only brought out for the priests to study and read from.

The writing on the scroll in Ezekiel's hand was messy, written all over and on both sides. This was no official record, but one of Ezekiel's own, rambling, untidy outpouring of phrases and sentences, jumbled together, defaced by blots and scratching-out, the product of one of those periods, when, as his contemporaries kindly put it, he'd been 'under the influence'! Bits of it illegible, as if his stylus had been unable able to keep up with the thoughts tumbling higgledy-piggledy out of his bursting head and his agonized heart. Impassioned. Irrepressible. Earnest. Awful.

Ezekiel was into writing. It was known that sometimes he'd lock himself away for days on end to put his thoughts on tablets or parchment. In that, he was quite different from Jeremiah, who was suspicious of a written scripture, which others could twist and misinterpret afterwards. Literal readings distort. Written words must be re-imagined spoken.

How can you say, 'We are wise,
we have the law of the Lord,' Jeremiah had taunted,
'when scribes with their lying pens have falsified it?'

On the banks of the Tigris, and with great show, Ezekiel unrolled his scroll and started to read from it; heavy stuff, dirges, laments and words of woe; good for the burial of the dead, but not much cheer in what was effectively, if not literally, a prisoner of war camp!

Even if they didn't like what they heard, they still listened to him, not because he was a priest, but because he was a prophet. There was never any shortage of priests to don the white turban and wear the long, patterned stole. Prophets, though, were a rare breed. Their authority stemmed from the belief that they spoke divine truth, borne out by events. They seemed to have an intimacy with the Most High that was as unnerving as it was uncanny.

For all his uncompromising messages, however, Ezekiel was beginning to be troubled by a flaw in his argument. While what he proclaimed was true (that their present plight was because they had sat so lightly to the values that had set them apart from the nations around them, treating their particular God in an offhand way), it still left them in an intellectual and theological no-man's land, that a landless people is a Godless people.

Ours is a different anxiety. It is the loss of meaning that comes with a loss of story. Even among the non-religious, there is a growing unease that we in the West are losing the key to understanding who we are and where we've come from, as our Judeo-Christian roots become increasingly unfamiliar to successive generations.

When the writer and poet, Harry Eyres, struck up a conversation with a young couple during a London tube journey, he was taken aback to discover they'd never heard of Adam and Eve. 'When I recounted the creation story in Genesis,' he recalls, 'one of them said, "Oh, it sounds like some religious thing."'

It struck Eyres afterwards that, that 'we had undergone a cultural revolution', which was no 'less far-reaching in its effects' than the one in China in the twentieth century, or, we might add, the one that engulfed the Hebrew exiles in the sixth century BCE.

Eyre's concern is that, 'In multicultural Britain', where 'education rightly stresses the diversity of traditions,' inter-cultural acknowledgement 'should not happen at the expense of the founding traditions of the society, the traditions of Greco-Roman thought, art and literature and Judeo-Christian religion and theology.' Without knowledge of those, Eyres wrote, 'very little else in the cultural and literary history makes sense. Ignorant of those things, a young person will walk through the great gardens of our culture, the Uffizi or the Prado or the National Gallery, the works of Dante, Shakespeare, Cervantes, Goethe, without being able to name the flowers.'

Chagall's Ezekiel is one such flower. Ezekiel may not have been alone in the world at that time in stumbling upon the idea of monotheism to solve his people's problem, but exile had made it all the more necessary. One universal God, who is over all and in all. He changed the story to keep the meaning. It might still have been limited to a rather petulant: 'Our God is the only God, and your Marduk is no God', but it began to enlarge human understanding in quite a profound and lasting way.

If meaning is similarly to be recovered for us, it will require a reinterpretation of the story of which Ezekiel is such an integral part, so that we can again name the flowers that have shaped our Judeo-Christian beliefs.

A Secular Future

On the banks of the Tigris, after Ezekiel had pronounced the last woe, the people watched fascinated and fearful, as their respected priest and puzzling prophet wound up the scroll and did the most incredible thing. He started eating it! Spectators, they still gagged on the papyrus by proxy, spellbound as they savored the moist parchment masticated to an indigestible pulp! Scrolls weren't consumed like cakes of *mazzoh*! Or digested like *challah* bread!

O man, swallow this scroll I give you, and eat your fill.

It seemed as if the sun had crossed from one side of the market square to the other before it was all over. An old wag in the crowd broke the tension, shouting: 'Taste good, did it, Ezekiel? Recommend it as a snack for starving canal diggers?!'

'It tasted as sweet as honey', was all he replied. Deflated, they drifted away in ones and twos, shaking their heads in bemused disbelief, the more practical to speculate on how Ezekiel's wife would cope when he started moaning and groaning from the pains in his stomach in the middle of the night!

The more thoughtful turned it over in their minds, recalling the psalm,

The Lord's judgments are true and righteous every one,
more to be desired that gold, pure gold in plenty,
sweeter than honey dripping from the comb.

On the day Ezekiel stood before his people eating the scroll, he was still poised between a religious past and a secular future. It was still a 'to be or not to be' for his people in exile. But he was beginning to sense, too, that that was not enough, because it had nothing to say to them where they were now. If they could only be the people of their Hebrew God on the banks of the river Jordan, what hope had they of ever being reunited with their God on the banks of the river Tigris?

It would only be later that he would be able to introduce them to a spirituality of hope; a spirituality than spanned their religious past and made sense of their uncertain future. He would do it by moving them on from their obsession with 'Why?': 'Why it had happened'; to seeing the greater need to answering 'How?' How they could still be the people of God in a vastly changed world. How it was possible to believe that God still cared.

This, though, would only come about when what was left of their religious past had collapsed totally, freeing prophet and people to move on. It happened when the puppet administration Nebuchadnezzar had installed in Jerusalem rebelled, with fatal results. The Babylonian response was swift, brutal and absolute: the city walls razed to the ground, the Temple demolished, and Zedekiah, the victor's vassal replacement as king (having had his eyes put out), taken in chains back to Babylon. It marked the end of everything they had pinned their hopes on, and which had defined their nationhood: Land, Monarchy, Temple.

In its place, Ezekiel was to offer them a spirituality that drew on, but that had also moved on from, their religious past, and that avoided the secular future they feared. It was a gradual revelation that came to him in that uncomfortable place, between water and water, between the Jordan of his homeland and the Tigris of their exile.

Many generations after the restoration that Ezekiel had prophesied had been fulfilled, another Jew who was more than a prophet, was baptized in the Jordan of their hopes. His was a message that spirituality was not some religious ark into which people needed to be rescued, but more like wheat and yeast, to be transformed by fire and water, into something quite different, but nourishing and deeply satisfying.

*

Of the two rivers encircling the town with which this chapter opened, the Ystwyth, as its name in Welsh implies, is a meandering runlet, spouting lazily out of fissures in the massive Pumlumon mountain range, a thousand feet above sea level. From there it saunters nonchalantly downwards towards the harbor, picking up speed and arriving in a bit of a rush and fluster! The Rheidol, on the other hand, is a pushy waterway, its name close to the Welsh for 'must'. It stems from a source far higher up and harsher than the Ystwyth's. It's a river that forces its way over waterfalls and a dam to thunder in a soapsuds swirl into the ocean floor below.

For Ezekiel, the faith they'd practiced in Jerusalem had been far too meandering, while the challenge of Babylon was that it was dangerously confident. It would take time for him to realize that God was in-between: neither with the old Jerusalem order, nor with the brash new civilization that was part of their lives in Tel-abib.

2. Between Religion and Atheism

Like shining from shook foil
Gerald Manley Hopkins

Who knows how many people are genuine atheists? That is people who have thought it through and come to the conclusion that there is no God – period; people for whom the caption on the London buses says it all: 'There's probably no God. Now stop worrying and enjoy your life'.

The novelist, Philip Pullman adopts a more thoughtful attitude, asserting,

> Even though I believe there is no God, that doesn't stop the questions I ask being religious questions ... questions about life and fate and meaning and purpose and all that sort of stuff. I think they are important.

While many may find themselves in sympathy with Pullman's position, they might still want to keep the door open to the possibility of God. They may be able to stack up a list of arguments that tilt the balance against the probability of God, at least in the commonly held view of what 'godness' should be about, but they are reluctant to pronounce the case closed. They hold back from pronouncing sentence that there's nothing there. They are on middle ground, between the two rivers of atheism and religion.

The twentieth century Czech playwright and statesman, Vaclav Havel, believes we may be 'the first civilization in the history of mankind that is completely atheist'. For Havel, 'human existence now isn't metaphorically anchored in any way in a code of moral conduct, from which we could then derive a moral code'. Maybe not in any obvious sense. The basis of the argument in this book, however, is that spirituality now provides the metaphor.

The writer, Edward Thomas, one of the Great War poets, who described the English countryside in prose and poetry of unrivalled beauty and perception, called himself an agnostic, but when he was killed in France in 1917 a diary entry for the previous week read, 'I never quite understood what was meant by God'. At other times Thomas said he wanted 'religion', and wrote in a way that strikes a modern reader as profoundly spiritual. In his reflection on friendship, in *The Style*, Thomas muses:

Things will happen which will trample and pierce, but I shall go on, something that is here and there like the wind, something unconquerable, something not to be separated from the dark earth and the light sky, a strong citizen of infinity and eternity. The confidence and ease had become a deep joy; I knew that I could not do without the Infinite, nor the Infinite without me.

Super-Sensible Realities

Our perception of the probability of God is affected by a number of factors, some almost tangential, others more substantial.

The two most commonly attested are the scientific revolution and the problem of evil, both of which surface in a couple of contemporary novels, published within a decade of each other around the turn of this third millennium.

In the one: *'Cadw dy ffydd, brawd'* by Owen Martell, we are introduced to Dafydd, approaching forty, having a bit of a midlife crisis, and wanting to believe, but finding that the faith he's been brought up on doesn't square with what he knows of the origins of life.

As Dafydd catches sight of Canada's snow-clad landscape during a flight over the North Atlantic, it jolts him into a romantic reverie on the difference it could make to him, not only to believe in a Creator God, but in an interventionist God too, a God who had a particular and a personal plan for his life. So he yearns to 'feel the Greatness and the Glory, and all those things that begin with a Capital Letter. Wouldn't it be great to believe,' he thinks, not in some tit for tat way, but with a 'genuine faith. Actually to believe. Really to know'. It's the cry of everyone suspended between religion and atheism who feels hoist on the petard of the Enlightenment's scientific method as the only source of knowledge.

Believing, though, is a different kind of knowing to scientific understanding, though the two are often confused. As rational creatures, we know, as Dafydd knows, that our world was not created in the six days of the Hebrew myth in Genesis chapter one. We know it is no longer the unique and sole creation of our early attempts to make sense of the world around us and the sky above us. Rather, it's a knobbly little planet orbiting round a not particularly special fireball in a solar system that is one of many, in a Milky Way galaxy, in a cosmos which may, or may not, stretch to infinity.

Let light come into being, and it does, not because of the direct fiat of some First Principle, but from ninety-three million miles away in eight minutes flat! And it will keep on coming until our particular star slowly expands into a Red Giant, and engulfs all the inner planets. But that's billions of years away, anyway! And there are some one hundred billion other galaxies in the universe, and who knows what other life forms exist out there? We don't need to understand the science to realize that information on this scale has had, and continues to have, a profound impact on how we define who we are, and what our relationship with others could and should be.

From the late seventeenth and early eighteenth centuries CE onwards, individualism, not authority, has became the defining mark of progress in Europe: reason, not myth. Science came into its own. God, as previously understood, is superfluous as an explanation for why things are and how things are. We now have the means to find out and to make discoveries that can explain things without the need for any 'Holy Other' to account for gaps in our knowledge. We have grown up. We need no longer be prey to the fears and forces that have kept humankind in subjugation to witch doctors and priests since time immemorial.

The creation stories of the Hebrew Scriptures, the Babylonian Epic of Creation, with their variants in every other faith, have been overtaken by empirically tried and tested knowledge. We are no longer in thrall to gods and goddesses to account for the salvaging of the components of life from some primordial chaos and of land emerging from the surrounding waters. We know from observation and by deduction that it was part of a natural process.

It was Charles Darwin, probably more than anyone else, who brought home the implications of this revolution to the populace at large, because it was about 'me' rather than 'it'; about biology rather than physics; about humankind, the animal kingdom and the plants, rather than the planets and the stars.

When Darwin published his theory of natural selection, *On the Origins of Species*, it touched the lives of ordinary people in an unprecedented way; it gave them the tools with which to challenge the previously unquestioned authority of Scripture and Church, even if that had not been the intention. Darwin wanted a scientific debate; a debate that engaged with the science of his work, not its knock-on effect on religion. Nevertheless, there was no escaping the theological challenge.

Darwin concluded:

There is a grandeur in this view of life, with its several powers, having been originally breathed into a few forms or into one; and that, whilst this planet has gone cycling on according to the fixed law of gravity, from so simple a beginning endless forms most beautiful and most wonderful have been, and are being, evolved.

It was only in a second edition, and in the face of a growing religious backlash unable to separate 'knowledge' from 'knowing', science from spirituality, that he expanded his conclusion to read: 'having been originally breathed *by the Creator* into a few forms or into one...'

For Darwin, the science was self-validating. The gloss should have been unnecessary. Surprisingly, it is a debate that has still got a lot of energy in it, with creationist lobbies on both sides of the Atlantic making a pitch for the Old Time Religion, and choosing to ignore Darwin's thesis that, 'It is not the strongest who survive or the most intelligent, but the ones most responsive to change'. These lobbies cannot ultimately succeed, though it may distort the learning of some for some considerable time.

'Knowing' is the language of spirituality, it describes 'those attitudes, beliefs and practices which animate people's lives and help them to reach out towards super-sensible realities'. The definition is that of the *New Dictionary of Christian Theology*. 'Super-sensible realities' take what we know and raise them to a different order of perception, where we catch a glimpse, where we sense the shadow, of some other reality that touches us at the deepest points of our lives.

It is what the Northumbrian writer, Bridget Hewitt describes as:

... an in-between land; a land without clear borders, with misty, uncertain edges; a land of infinite possibility. It's a land of story and strange tales: tales of seas parting to allow escapes from slavery, of burning bushes not burnt, of water turning into wine, of glorious visions on mountain tops... It's a land conjured in the hidden-ness of poetry, in the nuances of music, the magnificence of great vistas, the fragility of beauty and friendship.

For Ezekiel, exile had had the equivalent effect to the theory of evolution. It challenged cherished assumptions and unsustainable premises. It would lead eventually to the discovery that God has always operated in 'a land without clear borders', actually and metaphorically.

It is easy to slip into a deferential piety and to suspend one's critical faculties in the presence of writings hallowed by time and usage in each and every faith's scriptures; to forget that behind the texts as we have them today, edited, copied and translated, individuals, and sometimes whole communities, were engaged in huge internal struggles. These were dark nights of the soul brought on by external events, and marking seismic shifts in understanding.

Tempest will follow upon tempest and rumor upon rumor. People will pester a prophet for a vision; there shall be no more guidance from a priest, no counsel from elders.

As Ezekiel walked along the byways of Babylon, sometimes alone, sometimes with a few insightful companions, these were the unsettling thoughts that would not go away and that made his soul ache. When he jostled through this alien city's narrow street, or passed the monuments celebrating the conquests of its kings, from Naboplashar to Nebuchadnezzar, when he observed its traders confidently hawking their silks and spices, or watched the hardened locals puffing pensively on their bubble pipes, he wondered if they too asked similar questions of their gods.

Then:

In the twelfth year of our captivity, on the fifth day of the tenth month, a fugitive came from Jerusalem and reported that the city had fallen.

'God is no more,' he might well have shouted in anguish at the unresponsive sky. At least not God as he and they thought that they knew God. It was because Ezekiel was eventually able to find a way through this crisis of faith – to contribute to the rebuilding of his nation when Babylon itself was eventually invaded by the Persians, and the exiles permitted to return – that he has become such a source of inspiration to succeeding generations. What Ezekiel offered was not a restoration to the earlier faith, but a refinement of it in which the question that mattered was not 'why?', but 'what do we now need to become?'

If faith was to be rebuilt in a people who had lost their land (that most basic mark of national distinctiveness) and their temple in which their God had dwelt, as once God had hovered over the waters at the dawn of time, then it called for a different understanding of God, and a different understanding of the world.

Faith will always be concerned with a different question to that which engages the scientist. It was the great mistake of the past, from the time of Galileo to Darwin, to expect that the church could be the sole arbiter of what was true and what was false. In its arrogance, it placed itself where only God can be. Faith probes 'super-sensible realities'; it complements, not contradicts, science.

Darwin wrote that 'there is a grandeur in this view of life'. It was left to Gerald Manley Hopkins, the poet priest, whose life overlapped with Darwin's later years, to give it theological expression:

The world is charged with the grandeur of God.

It will flame out, like shining from shook foil;
It gathers to a greatness, like the ooze of oil
Crushed.

Great Wings Moving About Me

The main character in the second novel: *'yn hon bu afon unwaith'*,
by the poet-priest, Aled Jones Williams, is Tom. What gets in the
way of believing for Tom is that 'God and life's filth don't match'.

When Tom meets up, one last time, with Rhiannon, with
whom he's had a long and distracting affair, they both know she
hasn't long to live. They talk about end things mostly. As they
both gaze out to sea, Tom, who has a way with words as a
literary man, reflects wistfully that his lack of belief doesn't
prevent him feeling 'some longing, some yearning for someone
or something more than me. Someone who could lift me
tenderly, and place me like a flimsy particle, in the tiny corner of
a snowflake's intricate pattern'. It's a simile that lingers in the
mind. It's an image of such exquisite tenderness and imagination
that it perfectly describes the 'neither religious nor atheist', that
so many feel themselves to be.

'Life's filth' is a big issue whether it's put in the form of
questions: Why do bad things happen to good people? Why do
the innocent suffer? Or as a proposition: that the problem of evil
raises uncomfortable questions about the existence of a good
God.

Few things succeed in putting people off believing, more than
facile answers to the problem of evil, even when sincerely
expressed and obviously well-meaning. Caroline, was at a loss to
explain to her surviving son that he'd had a brother, called
Joseph, who'd been stillborn. 'I simply say that God was short of
an Angel and Joseph was chosen; it's what I believe'. Or the
leader of a women's meeting, who was equally at a loss, intro-
ducing prayers for the parents of a baby who'd died in his sleep,
by saying, 'It's because God had need of him'.

With the best will in the world, these kinds of answers just will not do, and we need to question them, as kindly as we can, every time they rear their muddled heads. We may not be able to offer the telling and convincing riposte, but that is no excuse for not challenging half-baked distortions that in the end don't help, because they don't satisfy, and ultimately make a nonsense of any grown-up faith.

That so many people accept such explanations, apparently unquestioningly, is quite worrying. It is as if, once they enter religious premises or join in religious activities, or slip into the religious default mode, they allow themselves to be inured to the rational thought they bring to everything else in their lives.

Natural disasters (tellingly termed as 'acts of God' by wily actuaries), are another area that test the tension between an ordered and an unpredictable world, sometimes to breaking point and beyond. What kind of God allows such things to happen: disasters, like the Indian Ocean tsunami that killed over two hundred thousand in 2004; or the earthquake that flattened Haiti's capital, Port-au-Prince, in 2010 with a similar loss of life, and made over a million homeless; or famines because the crops have failed as a result of too much or too little rain. It matters not whether the cause is climate change or the effects of ill-conceived human exploitation.

What kind of a God stands back from creation to allow genetic abnormalities to shatter cherished hopes; or disease, sometimes of epidemic proportion, to ravage whole communities; or the suffering of the innocent and the vulnerable through human cruelty; or the proliferation of wars with those who survive, displaced and permanently scarred.

Maybe it is Auschwitz-Birkenau, or some other memorial to 'life's filth', that prompts the question, or sitting helplessly besides the bed of a loved one, perhaps of a child, or of an older person, diminished by sickness or frailty. How can you believe in a good God in such circumstances?

The question is one the Jews have never been able to avoid. Since the days of Ezekiel it has been passed through the prism of a succession of 'exiles', and today is probably somewhere between the more assured 'I-Thou' position of the Rabbi, Martin Buber, who thought and wrote in the shadow of The Shoah, and the more uncertain one of the Rabbi who explained to me recently that half her congregation didn't believe in God. They may have rejected the *Hashem*, the Nameless One, of their Hebrew Scriptures, but maybe more than appeared to be the case still harbored the promise that God might still be there for them, despite everything.

For the fictional Tom, 'god' (lower case) was 'a question mark, a punctuation mark, a sigh, an empty space, a cellar, a hole, mist on a peak, a horizon, an empty chair, emptiness, a half open door, anger, something rusting in the dark, an old lover you remember as on first meeting.' For Tom 'there was something in the word that perhaps couldn't be filled with meaning. Some emotional residue, something spare.' It suggests a spirituality that is restlessly unfulfilled, and some of it could well have come from the lips of Ezekiel in his darker moments.

'Curse God, and die!' Job's wife told him at the beginning of the troubles that eventually stripped him of everything he held dear: livelihood, relationships, health. And many do. Job ultimately had no answer to the problem of evil, but at least he didn't garble theological nonsense!

Ezekiel was no stranger to life's filth. He knew what invading armies did:

...they will strip off your clothes, take away your splendid jewelry, and leave you stark naked... they will stone you and hack you to pieces with their swords. They will burn down your houses...

One of my darker moments for confronting the problem of evil, was standing in a fenced-off field in West Beirut, in the Lebanon. The gnarled gatekeeper had begrudgingly unlocked the padlocked gates when he thought we might be German rather than British or American. Earlier, a recent spate of anti-Western demonstrations had brought the traffic to a standstill. On Serail Hill, her Britannic Majesty's deputy ambassador had advised against the visit.

The field was outside Sabra/Chatila, a refugee camp that had become a ramshackle township for third generation Palestinian refugees: a ghetto of jumbled alleyways concealing jumbled lives and dreadful memories, like the two long days when marauding pro-Christian factions had chased through its unplanned maze looking for terrorists, and raping as they went, leaving thousands dead, most of them women and children. Collateral damage in a proxy war waged by external powers, was the official explanation – a crime against humanity, in anybody else's book.

They buried their dead in unmarked graves in this field in West Beirut, the dusty grass uncut, the neglected trees still keeping a mournful vigil. It was hard to believe in God in a place like that. Lebanon's famous poet, Kahil Gibran, might have had it in mind, when he wrote:

And I came to the place where all the paths of Life meet,
There I fell a wounded prey before the face of despair.

There is no satisfactory answer to the problem of evil and to the suffering of the innocent. Ezekiel's explanation was to see it as a consequence of systemic national faithlessness. But he also offered them hope.

I shall take you from among the nations, and gather you from every land, and bring you to your homeland. I shall sprinkle pure water over you... I shall give you a new heart and put a new spirit within you; I shall remove the heart of stone from your body and give you a heart of flesh. I shall put my spirit within you...

Gibran's poem may have plumbed the depths of despair when initially confronted by the confusion of the place where all paths meet, and there are no obvious exits, no uncomplicated solutions, but it too ends on a different note. Because it was in, not despite, the place of despair, that faith fluttered past:

And it was there that I heard unseen great wings moving about me,
And as I turned my eyes I saw Thee
Standing before me as the cedar of God on Lebanon;
I knew thee because the light was in thine eyes,
And the motherly smile on thy lips.
You blessed me with a touch,
And whispered to my soul these words:
'Follow me child, I am thy guide,
I shall reveal what sorrow doth hide.'

It is the capacity of spirituality to reveal 'what sorrow doth hide'; that is its strength. It commends belief as found neither in the extreme of an unquestioned religion, nor the desolation of atheism, but in the middle ground of rational thought consecrated by 'a motherly touch'.

*

Apart from Ezekiel, few took the exile more to heart than the young king, Jehoiachin. After months of depression that none his wives had been able to lift, and sleepless nights in agonies of self doubt, Jehoiachin decided to confide in the prophetic priest. He felt he was close enough to him in age to be able to understand his position. Moreover, as Buzi's son, he judged he had the breeding and the background to be able to converse without deference preventing him from being candid. Following prayers at the end of Shabbat, he invited Ezekiel to walk with him in the gardens of the house that now served as his palace in exile.

After the usual formal exchange of greetings, polite enquiries about the family and any difficulties the priests might be having in pursuing their calling in these unwelcome and unusual circumstances, Jehoiachin got to the point:

'Why has this happened to us, Ezekiel? Why have I lost my kingdom? The people say it is because of my father's failures. They quote the proverb (not to my face, of course), but I get to hear about it: "Parents eat sour grapes, and their children's teeth are set on edge".'

The Queen Mother, who would hear nothing spoken against the memory of her late husband, Jehoiakim, would not have approved of her son in intimate converse with Ezekiel. To her mind, it was Ezekiel who was largely responsible for stoking up so much resentment against Jehoiakim and his reign. Hadn't he denounced the late King in language that would have had him arrested if they'd been back in Jerusalem? He'd called Jehoiakim a man of bloodshed and violence, who had turned his back on the commandments, obeying none of them:

> He feasts at mountain shrines, dishonors another man's wife, oppresses the poor in their need; he commits robbery, he does not return the debtor's pledge, he looks up to idols, and joins in abominable rites; he lends both at discount and at interest.

The Queen dowager considered that Ezekiel should look to himself, and to his fellow priests, for their own failure to keep their God on side and not try to blame Jehoiakim, who had given his people ten years of prosperity.

'Is that what the proverb means, Ezekiel?' Jehoiachin persisted. 'Are our teeth, my people's teeth, to be set permanently on edge because of my father's shortcomings? Is it foreordained?'

'Not so, sire. If you repent of your father's sins, and revert to the values of your grandfather, King Josiah, of ever blessed memory, God will take pity on us. The kingdom will be restored. The Temple will again become the throne of the Most High. It is possible to break the cycle. A new generation need not be bound by the failures of its forebears.'

The king was silent for quite a while. 'Let me think about that one, Ezekiel.'

'I shall pray for you, sire.'

'I need your prayers, my priest. But more, perhaps, I need your prophecy.'

Ezekiel bowed, and withdrew.

A Dimension of Depth

If the scientific revolution and the problem of evil are the two most commonly stated reasons for questioning the probability of God, religious extremism is unlikely to be far behind.

Whenever a horrific incident, committed 'in the name of religion', assails our sensibilities, many will, and do, say, that if this is what religion leads to, they want no part in it. For all the good bits about peace and forgiveness in every religion, if the other bits can produce so much terror and carnage, then, they will argue, and justifiably, there must be something wrong, not just with its perpetrators, but with religion itself – all religions. At least with atheism there's no get out. There's no room for claiming: I was acting in the name of my God, quoting chapter and verse from the scriptures to justify it.

The answer to any extremism is moderation, and moderation often demands compromise. What is it about compromise that seems to sit so uneasily on the shoulders of faith's stalwarts? In some Christian circles, compromise is almost tantamount to apostasy! I was brought up on sermons in which the very mention of 'Laodicea', a little town, now in Western Turkey's Lycus valley, famous for its tepid medicinal waters, was enough to make the moderating deviants in the congregation tremble in their pews!

In the New Testament book of the Revelation, words of regret and sadness are addressed to Laodicea's fledgling Christian community that read today more like a bad end of term report than a word of encouragement: 'I know what you are doing, you are neither cold nor hot. How I wish you were either cold or hot!' So bad, indeed, is their condition, that expulsion seems the only alternative! 'Because you are neither one nor the other, but just lukewarm, I will spit you out of my mouth.'!

Similar references can, of course, be found in the writings of other faiths, and they have reverberated down the millennia, bedeviling the perception of many yearning for an inclusive faith, denying them the safety of middle ground.

Laodicea was a favorite stop for traders from the East. There they could exchange their wool and cotton for the Roman Empire's wine and cattle, and relax in its gymnasium, or laugh at the comedies of Aristophanes in its theatre. It was also the place to take the waters, which was a godsend to those suffering from skin complaints, asthmatic conditions or the onset of arthritis. And for those whose treatment required a daily oral dose of the stuff, they just had to pinch their noses and swallow!

In the context of the time, when the emperor Vespasian and his successors were intent on persecuting the fledgling Christian sect, the letter to the church at Laodicea was intended to be a rallying cry to the wavering, like Shakespeare's 'Henry V', urging on his troops with a:

Once more unto the breach, dear friends, once more;...
Now set the teeth and stretch the nostril wide,

Hold hard the breath and bend up every spirit
To his full height.

Out of context, though, such warnings against moderation have had disastrous consequences. Anything that perpetuates extremism, however unintentionally, needs to be challenged for the simple reason that in-between is often a better place to be than either of two opposite and extreme wings. It's the moderates who save the day in the long run, who restrain the hotheads, who ensure breathing space for the vast majority, and who sustain the faith for the many.

When religion is suspect because of extremism, there is, therefore, such a thing as a ministry of moderation to be performed, which requires that compromise be reinstated in every faith as a fundamental doctrine of belief. It is in that process that spirituality has a critical part to play.

Spirituality means a lot of different things to different people, but in the sense it is being used in these pages, it is the 'in-between' without which there can be no proper understanding of what it means to have faith. This is not to advocate some wishy-washy, neither-one-thing-nor-the other, sitting-on-the-fence creed, but to fly the flag for a positive, affirming, healing expression of belief.

Every faith honors its martyrs, those who surrender their lives for their beliefs. It is when martyrdom crosses over into the terrorism of the suicide bomber, however, that sympathy is lost.

When Simon Phipps, later to become a much-loved bishop of Lincoln, was an industrial chaplain in Coventry, he was a great advocate of compromise as a Christian virtue: not unprincipled, but responsible, compromise.

Why does compromise always have to mean 'giving way on the things that matter most' to one? Or accepting 'standards that are lower than desirable'? Get back to its root meaning and you find the word is a compound of two other words, namely: 'to promise' or to 'send forth' (*pro-mittere*), and 'together' (*com*). When people make promises to each other, it is because they intend to get on with them. 'Promise' is the language of moderation; 'together' implies co-operation not conflict. Compromise should, therefore, be about reasonable behavior; it should be about consideration for others, and middle ground.

Middle ground is often better ground because it saves one from extremism, from the unswerving certainties that threaten on every side. It is middle ground that is best for nurturing spirituality, for providing the space between unthinking religion and an uncompromising atheism.

Ezekiel might not be an obvious candidate for promoting moderation, but in that he was willing to face the unthinkable, and to tell his compatriots that their God had actually abandoned the temple, where their particular Transcendent One was thought of as dwelling for all time, he created the spiritual space in which new ideas could begin to find their place; ideas like the universality of God:

The glory of the Lord left the temple terrace and halted above the cherubim. They spread their wings and raised themselves from the ground; I watched them go... The glory of the Lord rose up and left the city...

In his little book, *God on Monday*, a forgotten classic, Phipps wrote that,

The transcendent, thought of in terms of spiritual space fiction, of 'another' world 'somewhere else', terms prominent in so many hymns, certainly this notion needs to be bundled out with the bag and baggage of 'the God of the gaps' ...

But the transcendent, thought of as the dimension of depth we experience in situations of responsibility, where life calls for love, this idea of the transcendent seems to me wholly viable. At such points of responsibility, where love's demands push through, we can see infinite depths of demands in the situation, which imply infinite depths of response in us. Both the situation and ourselves acquire an added dimension.

*

I do not know if there is such a thing as the God-gene, or if some brains are hard-wired to respond more readily to ideas of God. I only know that if God is, then God is for all and not for the few.

I do not know why some of the most ethereal spiritual music has been produced by composers who describe themselves as un-believing, but I am grateful that their work has allowed my spirit to soar.

I do not know why some of the most spiritual and the most thoughtful people I know, find my believing strange, but I am glad of their friendship.

I do not know what it means to think of God against the immeasurable vastness of the universe, any more than I can account for the problem of evil on earth, but I think it must all be of a piece.

I do not know how some who say they believe as I believe, can behave in ways I find abhorrent, but I will walk with them as long as they will walk with me, as I will walk with God, and believe God walks with me.

I do not know how spirituality works, I only know that, for me, God helps make sense of life, and explains me to myself. I cannot define or explain who or why God is; I cannot imagine God, but I sense I can trace the characteristics of God in the man who was baptised in the Jordan and transcended all religions.

3. Between Your Faith and Mine

Gather us in, O Love that fillest all;
Gather our rival faiths within thy fold;
George Mattheson

After Laodicea, it is Mecca, Amritsa and the Sacred Ganges that beckon, because if spirituality is about the middle ground between religion and atheism, it is also about the middle ground between different faiths. And that's a very attractive proposition for a generation that is socially much less judgmental and more open to seeing the good in others.

To have to choose to follow one faith to the exclusion of all others seems perverse to many today, especially if it implies the others are less good, or even wrong! Is faith not a matter of praxis, of good practice, rather than of orthodoxy, of right belief? As one Christian volunteer at a coffee morning for the homeless remarked, 'Your view of the Eucharist doesn't matter as you serve cake!'

Today's spiritual pilgrims feel a greater affinity with Abou Ben Adhem in Leigh Hunt's poem than they do with Ezekiel. Ben Adhem, based on the eighth century CE Sufi saint and mystic, Ibrahim Bin Adham, wakes in the middle of the night to find an angel in his room, writing in a big gold book, 'the names of those who love the Lord'. Enquiring if his own name was there, Ben Adhem is put out to be told that it was not, but bounces back robustly:

'I pray thee, then,
Write me as one who loves his fellow men.'

The angel wrote, and vanished.

The poem draws on an Islamic belief that on 'The Night of Records', in the month of Sha'ban, Allah opens the golden book of humankind and crosses off the names of those he loves and whom he is calling to him in the coming year. Ezekiel or Ibrahim, does God not love them equally? And when they pray is it not to the one God, though one may call him Allah, the other Hashem?

> The next night
> It came again, with a great awakening light,
> And showed the names whom love of God had blest,
> And lo! Ben Adhem's name led all the rest.

To imply an equality of faiths, however, is to tread on uniquely sensitive ground; and in the end is unhelpful. I write as one for whom the uniqueness of Christ has been, and continues to be, the key that unlocks my understanding of the nature of God and of the glory of human kind. For my friends, Salim, Nighat and Robina, however, it is to Muhammad (Peace Be Upon Him) that they look, as the last of the prophets, and in the Holy Qur'an they see a definitive text which both confirms and corrects the understanding of the Jewish and Christian Scriptures. While for my Jewish friends, Judith and Laura, Alan and Colin, the Messiah is still awaited.

Other friends, whose traditions are not monotheistic, hold to different positions which seem equally non-negotiable. Middle ground, therefore, is not necessarily common ground. Of course there will be some overlap of perceptions, some shared feeling after the Divine, but middle ground is more about the space where we can hear the resonances of each other's faith, and hopefully have others hear ours. It is more like the confidence of lovers, secure in the uniqueness of their relationship, who are not jealous of each other's friendships. Rather, because of the richness of their separate affections, they are able to bring something extra to the way they see and understand each other. In their love of, and with, each other, they can afford to be inclusive of others, because the love they share is anchored in a particular faithfulness.

That the Saddiqis were Muslims was immaterial when it came to sharing their grief over the senseless killing of Aamir, their seventeen-year-old son, on their own doorstep. These were friends, and their family tragedy affected ours, their sorrow became ours too. In our shared humanity, and as parents, Iqbal and I, Parveen and my wife Denise, embraced each other in a piercing wordlessness.

Conscripting Others into Our Vision of Reality

Middle ground can also be the place to share stories, to listen to different answers to the 'why?' all things have come to be, to awaken our curiosity, and, perhaps most important of all, in the current climate of our inter-dependence globally, of the realization that we cannot afford for our faiths to keep us apart.

In the 1990s, Samuel Huntingdon, a Harvard political scientist, argued the opposite, suggesting that too close an inter-mingling would lead to a clash of civilizations. It was an argument that chimed in with the political culture of America at the time, and seemed to be corroborated by the terrible attack in 2001 on New York's twin towers by Islamist extremists.

But such a perception was gradually, and thankfully, seen to be a dangerous course, leading to further alienation. Huntingdon's thesis effectively built a wall between east and west, between Christianity and Islam; a Creedal Curtain that would soon become impenetrable unless it was quickly dismantled, and by its very existence would lead to an increase in suspicion and mistrust.

Reflecting on the terrorist attacks on the twin towers, the Archbishop of Canterbury, Rowan Williams, who happened to be at a meeting in Trinity Church a couple of blocks away that fateful day, offered this measured response:

> Recognizing common experience is the exact opposite of using someone else to fit with your agenda, using them to play out roles you have worked out and assigned. We have been very resourceful in this over the centuries. Christians have conscripted Jews into their vision of reality, and forced them into a role that has nothing to do with how Jews understand their own past or current experience – what one scholar called 'using Jews to think with'. In the Middle Ages, Muslims too were made to play a part in the drama written by Christians, as a kind of diabolical mirror-image of Christian identity, worshipping a trinity of ridiculous idols.

Those were courageous words, especially while emotions were still raw, but they are a warning of what can happen when middle ground is conceded to the extremism of the wronged as much as of the wrongdoer.

Without recognition of middle ground, 'there will be bigger chaos, and you will not be able to stop it'. The speaker was an Indian student from Mumbai, on a scholarship to the UK to study journalism. 'I have been meeting Christian groups,' Basit explained at a Christian/Moslem conference we were both attending, 'because I like communicating with people and researching' and he was planning to meet at least once with most of the churches in his area. Problems of a religious nature exist, according to Basit, 'because people are short-sighted and narrow-minded.'

For this enquiring student from Mumbai, which had itself recently been the scene of a terrorist atrocity, inter-faith marriage seemed a practical contribution to improved harmony between the different races and cultures. 'Marriage will strengthen the bonds between communities,' he explained. 'No one will lose, everyone will gain, and many lives will be saved, not only in the United Kingdom and India, but around the globe.'

Certainly, inter-faith marriages can provide fruitful ground for respecting deeply held but different beliefs. Nevertheless, in his celebrated poem, 'On Marriage', Khalil Gibran writes of the necessity for maintaining middle ground if the identity of the one is not to be subsumed by the other:

...Let there be spaces in your togetherness,
And let the winds of the heavens dance between you...
Fill each other's cup but drink not from one cup.
Give one another of your bread but eat not from the same loaf.

Marriage had undoubtedly opened the door to greater understanding between different faiths for Ruth, a Methodist local preacher and a former Primary School head. Ruth's marriage to Raj, a Malay Sikh, had been a seventeen-year-long love story. After Raj's death from an aggressive cancer, Ruth fondly recalled how he'd told almost everyone they met, 'Always be grateful to God and to each other, for every moment, every second of every day. Life is precious.' Both found their own spirituality enriched and enlarged through the faith of the other.

In bereavement, Ruth drew on her Christian experience of incarnation and resurrection to affirm that, 'God is with us in whatever the daily "stuff" of life is for us.' After a service of thanksgiving in the local ecumenical church in Milton Keynes, where both had felt they belonged, Ruth took Raj's ashes back to Malaysia, where they were blessed at the Gurdwara before being scattered at sea in the traditional way.

It is in real life stories such as these that we see the sense and the blessing of a spirituality that is not some esoteric pursuit, but the living out and the loving of being together on middle ground, and finding God already there.

Sing and dance together and be joyous,
but let each of you be alone,
Even as the strings of a lute are alone
though they quiver with the same music.

The challenge for middle ground is often how to handle the sticking points of one's own faith, as well as of the faith of the other. For some, it may be possible to revisit and to reinterpret, without losing what's special and precious and sacred about each. For others, the idea of two or more 'great luminaries' may be a bridge too far. Maybe the very contemplation of it will imply a dismantling of what makes that faith unique.

While, therefore, inter-faith marriages are on the increase, certainly in the Western hemisphere, they can often seem to be beset by more problems than possibilities. The country in which the couple ends up living may pull the relationship in ways neither partner had anticipated in the first flush of romantic love. In which faith are any children to be raised? What expectations are there for the care of elderly relatives?

Acknowledging these and other difficulties, the Sri Lankan Methodist minister and onetime professor of ecumenical theology in Drew University, New York, S. Wesley Ariarajah, nevertheless, believes they are not insurmountable if the religions concerned accept that these inter-faith partnerships are a modern reality rather than an unfortunate aberration or even betrayal. 'We need a theology that can interact with other ways of believing and being,' he says. 'More than anything else, we need a theology that makes us hospitable. An inhospitable theology cannot produce hospitable people.'

Nothing is gained by laying down hard and fast ground rules for dialogue. Instead, it is in the listening, and, perhaps more, it is in the silences between us that understanding comes. It is not about setting out to change the other, but to be changed oneself in the encounter, and to be surprised by a God who refuses to fit into any of our neat categories. 'If you truly believe your religion comes from God,' Tenzin Gyatso, the fourteenth Dalai Lama reminds us, 'then you have to believe other religions are also created by God.'

A hundred years earlier, the influential Scottish parish minister and writer of theological and devotional works, George Mattheson, had been very much a voice before its time with his hymn (which seems to be suspiciously absent from too many contemporary hymn books!):

Gather us in, O Love that fillest all;
Gather our rival faiths within thy fold;
Rend each one's temple veil, and bid it fall,
That we may know that thou hast been of old.

Gather us in—we worship only Thee;
In varied names we stretch a common hand;
In diverse forms a common soul we see;
In many ships we seek one spirit land.

In 2006 CE, Glasgow University convened a unique series of dialogues on Islam and Inter-Faith Relations, with contributions from Jewish, Christian, Hindu and Buddhist scholars. It was an academic attempt to address the challenge that, 'under radically changed conditions, tradition needs to be transformed or otherwise it is in danger of ending up as a museum piece, nicely preserved but essentially dead.' The dialogue proceeded on the premise that, 'In each religion people feel the need to clarify how they understand and assess other religions from within their own faith and whether they may have to reconsider the self-understanding of their own religion within the light of an increased and deepened knowledge and understanding of the others.'

It paralleled less academic approaches where a handful of people from different faiths meet regularly in each other's homes to share the experience of living their beliefs in relation to a comparable phrase from each of their sacred texts, inspired by Focolare spirituality. Or the practice of Abrahamic Scriptural Reasoning, where Jews, Christians and Muslims, clergy and lay, academics and scriptural novices come together to explore and to share interpretations of each other's sacred texts. These are not Damascus Road encounters, like the one where Saul of Tarsus, the rabid Pharisee, became Paul the pioneering Christian Apostle, but a deepening of insight into the sheer wonder of God, and an emotional understanding, rather than just one of the intellect, of what makes the other tick, and why.

> And stand together, yet not too near together.
> For the pillars of the temple stand apart,
> And the oak tree and the cypress
> grow not in each other's shadow.

At the very time Huntingdon was working on his faith-based separatist model for different power blocks, another American academic was doing similar research, specifically into the global distribution of the Christian faith, and coming up with a confidence-based, rather than a fear-driven, model for inter-cultural, inter-faith co-existence. By showing the transformation of Christianity into a predominantly non-Western, non-White faith, Philip Jenkins, a professor of history and religious studies at Penn State University, painted a picture that had consequences for all faiths.

The reality now is that whatever the predominant faith of a particular country, there will be other faiths present, and the stability of those societies will depend not on suppression or containment of minority faiths, but on mutual respect, and a genuine attempt to understand and to appreciate the other, to detect the voice of God in the other, and to pursue a thoughtful, caring life with the other.

Jenkins invites us to,

Imagine the world of the thirteenth century armed with nuclear warheads and anthrax. In responding to this prospect, we need at a minimum to ensure that our political leaders and diplomats pay as much attention to religions and to sectarian frontiers as they ever have to the distribution of oilfields.

The world is too dangerous a place to allow us to use religions to wage our wars, rather than to see in them the resources that can enable us to build bridges and to bring peace with each other.

Trans-located by a Forelock

One of the most startling passages in Ezekiel describes his 'trans-location' from exile in Babylon back to Jerusalem, occasioned a kind of out-of-body experience in which the individual becomes convinced that he or she has been transported to another location whilst still being bodily present in the same place. In his vision, instead of a people sobered and ennobled by defeat, but still faithful to the old religion, Ezekiel found an increasingly plural-istic society.

So this sensitive, passionate man, in his mid-thirties, full of what we'd call evangelical fervour, is confronted by what he sees as the worst excesses of syncretism, of religious amalga-mation. It was his conviction that it was these very practices that had led to his people's moral degradation and initial defeat at the hands of Nebuchadnezzar. Six year later, instead of a people who had mended their ways, he's baffled and confused to find them even more deeply enmeshed.

On the fifth day of the sixth month in the sixth year, as I was sitting at home and the elders of Judah were sitting with me, suddenly I felt the power of the Lord God come upon me. I saw what looked like a man; from the waist down he seemed to be all fire and from the waist up to shine and glitter like brass. He stretched out what appeared to be a hand and took me by the forelock.

In exile, Ezekiel had idealized Jerusalem, its temple and its people, and was shocked to discover that, in his eyes, they had changed for the worse. Time had no more stood still for the ones left behind than for those taken away. Whereas the exiles had found themselves a minority in an alien culture and, therefore, with an added incentive to preserve their different and particular identity, the ongoing population had another reality to contend with, and to adjust to.

Life in Jerusalem and Judea had been allowed to go on very much as before. They had a different king, Zedekiah, a Babylonian puppet, and they paid higher taxes, but they still had access to their temple, even if, having been stripped of its most valuable treasures, it was now a shadow of what it had once been in its heyday. Deprived of the scheming of the exiled clerical and aristocratic elite, the Babylonians were banking on the priests that remained being relatively harmless. In time, they would discover that the new, younger set could be even more troublesome than the old!

Gradually, the occupying incomers had brought with them their foreign ways and their foreign gods; temple, city and country had become a lot more cosmopolitan. For some of the Judeans, it must have seemed like a liberation from the prescriptive practices and sanctions of a strict old faith.

In a vision from God a spirit lifted me up between earth and heaven, carried me to Jerusalem, and put me down at the entrance to the inner gate facing north, where stands the idolatrous image which arouses God's indignation.

A statue to Asherah now stood outside the temple's north gate, the troubling shapes of unfamiliar, unclean animals had been carved into its austere walls, and the fertility rituals of death and rebirth, of the cult of the Sumerian god, Tamumuz, had been incorporated into the life of a nation that had previously rested on the promise to Noah, that,

As long as the earth lasts,
seedtime and harvest, cold and heat,
summer and winter, day and night,
they will never cease.

Six years on, Jerusalem seemed a very different place from the one Ezekiel and his fellow exiles had left. An accommodation had set in between the rulers and the ruled, which was all too obviously reflected in these alien religious practices. It reached an apogee of awfulness for Ezekiel when he saw:

...there, by the entrance to the sanctuary of the Lord, between porch and altar, were some twenty-five men with their backs to the sanctuary and their faces to the east, prostrating themselves to the rising sun.

Which was worse, in Ezekiel's book? The apostasy itself, or the insult of showing their backsides to the God of Abraham, Isaac and Jacob?!

In an ecstatic fury, Ezekiel transposed his rage onto Judah's God, whom he describes wreaking indiscriminate vengeance on man, woman and child. It was possibly an image of what would befall them in further battles at the hands of temporal enemies. In predicting it, Ezekiel was perhaps initiating it too, in that strange concept that the prophet is privy to the thoughts of the Most High, and by announcing it, effectively makes it come to pass.

The modern reader has to handle the uneasy juxtaposition between the sublime, intense spirituality of Ezekiel, who helped shape the monotheism of his people, with Ezekiel's rather primitive picture of a God who appears to be more of a monster than a beneficent deity! The evolution of our understanding of God has been a gradual process, and we are by no means at the end of it.

In the meantime, we have to separate what is of its time, from what is timeless. Those who fail to do so, burden the present with the primitiveness of the past, and the value of scripture is distorted to become a 'savage text', according to Adrian Thatcher, professorial research fellow in applied theology at the University of Exeter. An uncritical approach to scripture, he warns, ends up making 'hatred holy', 'seekers after truth its jealous guardians,' and, worst of all, endowing its strictures with 'divine authority'.

Is it perhaps reading too much into the Gospel song:

When I fall on my knees
With my face to the rising sun,
O Lord, have mercy on me

that we see in these lines something that eluded Ezekiel, but which is part of the inheritance of Jesus of Nazareth five-hundred years later?

One God, World without End

What, then, of these twenty-five elders, singled out for such opprobrium by Ezekiel? What did they think they were doing? Had they, in fact, abandoned the faith of Abraham, Isaac and Jacob in favor of unfamiliar spiritualities; had they transferred their allegiance, lock, stock and barrel, to the sun god, whom they could at least see, who moved through the sky, who was the source of life and made the crops grow? Or might there be something more subtle going on here that Ezekiel, in the intensity and myopia of his vision, just could not see?

Might the twenty-five elders have been attempting to go down a different route, and to be worshipping God through the sun, without also abandoning their worship of the Nameless One; to be beginning the exploration that leads to the conviction that there may be many spiritualities, but there is only one God?

The common ground between these two positions is no easier to see now than it was then. These were, and still are, rivers apparently flowing in opposite directions, the one, fast and furious, the other slower, more measured, but equally intent on reaching the unfathomable sea.

It was a moment in the history of the world when monotheism, belief in one God, was beginning to capture the human mind. The Pharaoh Akhenaton's experiment in a single deity, some seven centuries earlier, had been short lived, and after his death the old practices and beliefs had been re-established. The monotheism emerging from the Hebrew tradition was more robust, and, in its turn, may have been a derivative of Akhenaton's Egyptian experience, filtered through Egyptian runaways who found refuge and sanctuary among the hill people of the upper Jordan. The one God idea had come to stay, and as far as Ezekiel was concerned there was no accommodating it to a variety of faiths. But that was not how the twenty-five elders saw it.

Unlike the exiles, they were not a minority in an alien culture. They were still on God's own land. If there were foreign gods and goddesses there too, it must be because their God had allowed it. Theirs was, therefore, a very different journey to that of Ezekiel's. Neither had got it right, neither Ezekiel nor the twenty-five Elders. In our third millennium CE we might not be getting it right, either, but not to try would be disastrous.

There is still a deep rooted fear of syncretism in the monotheistic faiths that reflects their journey from a seeming multiplicity of deities towards a single, clear 'Other'. But in their intent to block out what is strange and unfamiliar, monotheists might also be missing what might also be coming from God.

What was going on in and around the temple in Jerusalem, which Ezekiel saw and rejected, may not have been unlike that which confronts monotheistic believers when they encounter Hinduism. Ursula King, one-time Professor of Religion at Bristol University, cautions against too premature a judgment of what is strange and unfamiliar. In a British television series on the 'Lives of Jesus', presented by the erudite and ever generous Mark Tully, King interprets what is taking place in Vishnu's magnificent temple in South India. Vishnu, 'the source of the universe and everything in it, lies enthroned on the thousand-hooded serpent of eternity in the inner sanctuary'. 'Vishnu is at the center of this temple and in that central place,' King explains. 'It is almost like going into a Catholic Church and finding God hidden in the tabernacle above the altar'!

Among those who see God everywhere, in all faiths and none, in the trees and the streams, in the greater and the lesser lights of the firmament, in the seasons of the year and the orbit of the planets, there is equally a deep-rooted fear of the exclusivity of monotheism. In their openness to the God they see in everything, and who is everywhere, it was Ezekiel's fear that they could end up with a God who is nowhere and nothing.

A Harmony of Prayer

A thousand miles away, as distant culturally, spiritually and temporally, a cluster of twenty-first century Christians and Muslims met to pray in the contemporary chapel of Gladstone's Library in North-East Wales.

William Ewart Gladstone was a complex man; a would-be Anglican priest who became a great statesman; a Chancellor of the Exchequer who delivered thirteen budgets and was returned to power as Prime Minister four times. He possessed an amazingly broad outlook for an age commonly associated with Victorian prissiness; his extensive library stocked with works on Islam as well as on Christianity and other religions.

This particular inter-faith group of Christians and Muslims had developed a pattern for this most intimate of spiritual sharing in successive meetings over a number of years. To begin with, hesitantly, they'd prayed concurrently, in separate rooms.

In one room, standing in line and facing Mecca, Muslims called on Allah:

Allahumma antas-salam waminkas-salam, tabarakta ya thal-jalali wal-ikram
O Allah, You are As-Salam [the One free of all defects and deficiencies] and from you is all peace, blessed are You, O Possessor of Majesty and honor.

And in another room, standing in a circle, the Christians joined in this prayer of St Augustine of Hippo:

Lord, the house of my soul is narrow: enlarge it, that you may enter in.
It is ruined: O repair it! It displeases you: I confess it, I know.

Then both faith groups progressed to sharing the same space, observing each others' praying, and witnessing each others' praying; Muslims first:

Allahumma ma asbaha bee min ni'matin, aw bi-ahadin min khalqik, faminka wahdaka la shareeka lak, falakal-hamdu walakash-shukr,
O Allah, what blessing I or any of Your creation have risen upon, is from You alone, without partner, so for You is all praise and unto You all thanks.

Then the Christians:

> Loving God, Take our hatreds: make them into handshakes; take our prejudices: make them into peace-offerings. Take our arguments: make them into alliances; take our schisms: make them into songs.

But that morning it felt different.

As the February sun cracked open the darkness of night, letting it trickle tentatively across the misty Flintshire countryside, Robin, an Anglican priest, wondered whether, in-between the prayers of each faith, the group might this time pray in harmony.

The Christians would offer 'the Jesus Prayer': one of the oldest formulaic devotional exercises, widely used in the Eastern Orthodox tradition, where it has been taught and endlessly discussed. It is a prayer both of the heart and of the mind, each phrase to be repeated slowly, three times, until the words and the breathing gradually merge in a natural rhythm:

> Lord Jesus Christ, have mercy upon me, have mercy upon them, have mercy upon us, have mercy upon her, have mercy upon him.

The Muslims, from their own tradition, would pray:

> Astaghfirul-lah / I ask Allah for forgiveness; Astaghfirul-lah / I ask Allah for forgiveness; Astaghfirul-lah / I ask Allah for forgiveness.

Between the altar, with its simple hand-embroidered cloth, and the rows of chairs, they sat side by side, Christians and Muslims, cross-legged, shoes removed, on the plain polished floor. And, as they prayed, their prayers became as one, until it was impossible to distinguish the voices of one faith from those of the other: 'mercy and forgiveness'; 'forgiveness and mercy'; the pattern, tempo and intention of each faith's prayers corresponding to that of the other.

At the chapel's east end, a startling sculpture in clear and colored glass, a quartet of bold, blood-orange darts converging on a single, central, swirling circle, encouraged an attitude of inclusiveness in motion.

It was a moment, an experience, that transcended doctrinal differences and touched on the essence of every believer's relationship with God. As both reached out to God – the children of Allah, the followers of Jesus Christ – they felt themselves becoming, and to be extraordinarily close to God and to each other. It was a moment of revelation, of renewal; because of, and through the other.

In that place and at that time they had come very close to losing themselves in the one God who is over all and in all. In the words of Sheikh Abdulla, who was part of the group, and had been involved in and supportive of the process from its tentative beginning many years before: 'It testified to the Great Truth that we human beings were One Family; our father is Adam and our Mother is Eve (peace be upon them); and Our God is One.'

Explaining it afterwards to others who had not been there, who had not been transported in the spirit of that one God into the very presence of the Most High, would prove elusive, open to misunderstanding even.

For Robin, who had been the catalyst for that experience, poetry seemed the best way:

The lightening strike of the cross
Ripped the veil of the temple
In two; revealing, uncovering
the open space of shekinah,

in which my soul
sank to its knees
in the resonance of holiness,
unshackled, unveiled,
in the presence
of a common humanity.

As a place dedicated 'for the pursuit of divine learning', Gladstone's Library in the little village of Hawarden, a stone's throw from Chester, was not such an unlikely place for this meeting of faiths; its weathered sandstone walls enclosing a warmth and an openness that was consistent with, and conducive to, this transition from meeting together to pray, to meeting to pray together.

*

I cannot believe that when Muslims pray, and Jews pray, and Hindus pray, that the God I know as the Father of our Lord Jesus Christ does not receive them as generously as me.

And I know that if I had been born in India, as likely as not, I'd have been a Hindu or a Muslim or a Sikh. But it is Christianity that has made me what I am.

When Tolkien spun his tales of Hobbits, of *The Lord of the Rings* and *The Silmarillion*, he set them in Middle-earth: not at a physically distant time, but rather 'at a different stage of imagination'. Spirituality is a 'different stage of imagination' for the world's faiths, and if we have lost it we need to recover it, and if it is new to us we need to embrace it, because, as Bilbo Baggins sang in comfortable middle age: the road ahead eventually reaches the point 'where many paths and errands meet.'

4. Between Magic and Mystery

It guided me, this light
More surely than the light of noon
St John of the Cross

The irascible, likeable Bilbo Baggins is ideally placed to take us on to another stage in our journey, this time to Tolkien's magical world of the wicked wizard, Saruman, the ambivalent Gollum, and the ominous Sauron.

The message of the great monotheistic Faiths is that mystery is good, but magic is bad. Mystery safeguards the idea that God is difficult or impossible to understand or explain. Magic, on the other hand, conjures up visions of supernatural forces that are either indifferent to God or in open rebellion against God. Mystery is an awareness of the supernatural that bestows blessing. Magic is a harnessing of supernatural powers for selfish ends.

It was because that 'famous magician' and 'popular entertainer', at the time of the Acts of the Apostles, Simon of Samaria, had tried to buy what he saw the Apostles Peter and John do, when they conferred God's Spirit on the new converts by the laying on of hands, that he was so roundly condemned. God's gifts were not for sale! Mystery is given. Magic is grasped. Or is that too simplistic a distinction? Are not both open to misuse; have not both the potential to bless?

Ezekiel is the supreme example in early Hebrew belief of the God-fearing person who epitomizes the positive contribution of mystery. One of the great spiritual figures of all time, Ezekiel's spirituality is clothed in, and clouded by, almost unremitting mystery. His prophecies throughout originate in the most intense and often peculiar mystical experiences.

Though he never claimed to have seen God, he had heard God, and been shown the awesome paraphernalia that surrounded the Deity: living creatures, sparkling wheels with the power of sight, human likenesses, volcanic fires, dead bones walking. And in his mystical trances he had done irrational things: become mute, eaten parchment, cooked with feces, lain down for months on end bound and naked, and had out of body experiences, like the one when he was led:

> ...to the gate which faced east, and there, coming from the east, was the glory of the God of Israel. The sound of his coming was like that of a mighty torrent, and the earth was bright with his glory. The form that I saw was the same as I had seen when he came to destroy the city, the same I had seen by the river Kebar, and I prostrated myself.

It is extremely likely that some equally intense and exceptional individuals, who followed the cults of Babylon, had undergone parallel experiences and had similar visions, but Ezekiel would have branded them magical, and their recipients bad, or at best, misguided. The folk memory of King Saul, consulting a medium at Endor, prior to his defeat in battle at the hands of the Philistines, became the definitive cautionary tale for the Jews who survived the exile, that to dabble with what became known as spiritualism, as opposed to spirituality, spelt death. There was even a solemn injunction in the Torah against permitting a medium, a witch, to live.

Christianity absorbed this condemnation of the magical, while extolling mystery as the ultimate appellation for spiritual wonderment. So Christ's final ordeal is referred to as 'the mystery of the cross', his last meal as 'the mystery of the Eucharist', and his story re-enacted at Passiontide, from the backs of rickety handcarts in town market places and lofty Cathedrals alike, as 'mystery plays'.

Tis mystery all! [Charles Wesley sang.] The Immortal dies:

Who can explore His strange design?

For some (lay, religious and ordained), Christian discipleship was to lead them to expect to experience in prayer, rare Divine 'touches', possibly eventually attaining 'mystic marriage', and to savour similar insights to those given to Ezekiel, the most mystical of all the Hebrew prophets.

Christianity, therefore, takes mystery very seriously, and it is hard to better the description of the Christian mystical experience than in the writings of the sixteenth century CE monk, St John of the Cross, in his epic poem, The Ascent of Mount Carmel:

> It guided me, this light,
> More surely than the light of noon
> To the place where he
> Whom I knew well
> Waited for me,
> A place where there was
> No one to be seen!

In our own time many have also been inspired and challenged by the mystical works of the American Trappist monk and contemplative, Thomas Merton, of whom the Dalai Lama remarked, that it was the first time he 'had been struck by such a feeling of spirituality in anyone who professed Christianity.'

Merton's gift, like that of St John of the Cross, was to embody the positive value of mysticism in perfecting an experience of God that is refined to the nth degree, but still stays on the side of what is acceptable within the Judeo/Christian corpus of faith.

The Sufi stream serves a similar purpose in Islam, revealing the emotive, ecstatic side of the more austere and proscribed Qur'an. Its greatest luminary and exemplar was the thirteenth century CE mystic, Jalal al-Din Rumi. His was a call for his fellow Muslims to live beyond themselves, to transcend the mundane, even, and most controversially, Islam itself:

> What shall I do, O ye Muslims, for I do not know myself anymore
> I am neither Christian, nor Jew, nor Zoroastrian, nor Muslim...

Nevertheless, Islam, like its Jewish and Christian antecedents, will still have no truck with anything magical or demimonde.

While all three monotheistic faiths have, in their different ways, therefore, a reserved place for mystery and mysticism as providing a unique insight into the nature and being of God, magic and the magical remain firmly out of bounds. And yet a great many people in the West are finding their spirituality awakened and nurtured more by alternative beliefs and practices than by the mysticism of the great faiths.

Occulture

Christopher Partridge, formerly Professor of Contemporary Religion at the University of Chester, goes so far as to call this phenomenon a 'new spiritual awakening'; one that emerges 'from an essentially non-Christian religio-cultural milieu', that 'both resources and is resourced by popular culture', but is 'not at all alien to the majority of Westerners'.

This blend of contemporary culture and the occult, which he terms 'occulture', is nevertheless, in Partridge's view, still influenced 'by latent Christian belief.'

Its origins may lie in that 'vast spectrum of beliefs and practices sourced by Eastern spirituality, Paganism, Spiritualism,

Theosophy, alternative science and medicine, popular psychology,' including 'a range of beliefs emanating out of a general interest in the paranormal,' but 'more often than not, when these themes bubble to the surface in the West they carry an eclectic mix of occultural ideas and influences,' including some Christian beliefs.

If, therefore, the great faiths are not to part company with the large swathes of contemporary seekers after an authentic and living spirituality, at least in the current climate, some cross-over points will need to be established between them and these new 'believers'. Such meeting might even prove liberating for the faiths as well as enriching for the disciples of this new spiritual awakening.

The challenge and the opportunity of this current phenomenon are captured in a touching little vignette from a Methodist church in St Athan village on the Glamorganshire coast. With her unconventional lay husband, Dave, Deacon Michelle had initiated and developed something called 'Mosaic': a fresh expression of church for those with little or no previous church experience. One day, 'a colorful, extrovert woman with two children dropped by,' Dave recalled: 'a beautiful community member, who couldn't do or be enough.

'She prays, has encountered the Divine, but wouldn't class herself as a Christian. She certainly appreciated the Jesus way of being, but regards herself as a "post-modern Jedi Knight"! I think when she prays,' Dave conjectured, 'she must be using "the Force"', adding, 'how do you explain that to your average Conservative Evangelical?!'

To be fair, though, it's not just 'your average Conservative Evangelical' who might find that hard to swallow! It seems so totally alien to all that the great faiths have taught. Alien or not, it's where a very large number of Westerners now find themselves, holding to what Partridge calls, a 'de-tradition-alized Christian belief'.

St Athan, not far inland from the busy Severn Estuary, may be better known today as home to an air force base than for its woman saint, Tathan, who founded a church there in the sixth century CE. There is something challengingly contemporary, however, about St Athan still being a place of engagement between the faith 'once given', and the tribal resonances of a druidic age, repositioned as a fictional monastic order from a distant galaxy!

Where, then, is the in-between spirituality that can take this kind of situation in its stride? A spirituality that recognizes and wrestles with the pull of two rivers apparently flowing in opposite directions. The one: the tried and tested experience of traditional faith, where God is 'mystery', beyond and outside us, who presents us with the possibility of a better way of living and of loving, and whose austere and seemingly high expectations of humankind formed such a key element of Ezekiel's thinking. The other: a movement away from systems and dogma towards an acknowledgement of direct, individual experience, where the focus of faith becomes the self and, in so far as God can be known at all, is known only in terms of what we can feel and sense. That was also something that had become part of Ezekiel's journey of faith. Because, for him too, God had become real in the ecstatic and intensely personal experience of his visions. It was within himself that Ezekiel found the God he'd thought they'd lost.

Ours has become a society that leans more towards individual experience than to prescriptions of divine expectations, where the health spa has replaced church as the better place to 'ease your soul', endowed with almost 'magical' powers to rejuvenate and invigorate us. In Professor Partridge's language, our culture is less interested in 'the interior knowledge and experience of transcendent reality external to the self', and more interested in 'the turn to the self, or "subjectivisation"'. Ours, therefore, is a culture that finds the idea of a God apart from and outside of ourselves, who taps on the window of our lives wanting to be admitted and to bond with us, who has no claim on us, but who waits instead to be claimed by us, almost incomprehensible.

Between such two different spiritualities, where is God to be found? Is there an in-between spirituality that can hold both these positions in place by allowing each to inform, to amend and to enhance the other?

Someone touched me

There are clues in an insufficiently rated incident from the Christian Gospels where Mystery and Magic, the mystical and the subjective, converge in a startlingly unexpected way. When the itinerant Galilean preacher, Jesus of Nazareth, went from town to town preaching and healing, his reputation for homespun spirituality and acerbic wit struck a chord in an audience numbed by years of platitudes from hypocritical prelates and the brutality of Roman steel. His healings, too, were always more than spectacles. They implied that he was somehow special and his message of a New World more than a passing fad.

Among the crowd that particular day was a woman suffering from chronic uterine hemorrhaging. Hers was a double handicap. In addition to the pain and the humiliation, there was the social exclusion of the Levitical law, which rendered her ritually 'unclean'. To avoid further embarrassment, she'd decided to catch up with Jesus as far as possible from where she lived and was known. She'd already exhausted her investments on consulting different doctors, and her last chance was the Galilean 'shaman'.

And in case we are tempted to think that this is not faith, the Benedictine monk, Gregory Collins from Glenstal Abbey in County Mayo, in Ireland, cautions us to remember that, 'Faith is obscure, because compared to our normal, everyday knowledge, it is dark and imprecise. The contact with God that it yields is rather like the embrace of a lover in a darkened room. It is passionately real knowledge, of a tactile, immediate kind.'

It was not unusual, therefore, for the healing preacher to find himself at the center of an excited crowd, jostling to get as close to him as possible, to field their questions, to hear his answers. This occasion was different, though. This time he performed, what reads now like an *involuntary* healing. There's nothing like it in the canonical Christian corpus. No consent was sought or granted. It just happened, 'like magic'.

Jairus, who looked after the local synagogue, had asked for a healing for his sick daughter, and Jesus had agreed to go with him to the girl's bedside. He was on his way to her, teaching as he went, the crowd as thick and expectant as ever, when a woman in the throng edged her way forward, step by step, until she was just close enough to slip her anemic arm, incognito between the bulky frames of the fellows in the front. She could feel his coarse fabric in her feeble fingers.

> In the fortunate night [St John of the Cross]
> In secret, seen by none
> And seeing nothing
> Having no other light or guide
> Than that which burned in my heart.

The response in her body was electrifying. She sensed something had happened inside her: a physical sensation, searing. Years of discomfort, of shame, could be over. It was time to slip away to wait and see if it would last, to melt back into dusty anonymity and make her way back home to her children and her man, when the shaman stopped what he was saying, mid-sentence. 'I know someone touched me.' She tried to make herself even more inconspicuous. His words pounding to the beat of her heart: 'I felt my energy being used.'

Though this story occurs in all three synoptic Gospels, it is only in Luke, the Greek trained doctor, who provides that particular detail, encouraging speculation that the evangelist 'still worked within the idea of Hellenistic magic that regarded Jesus as possessing a kind of impersonal force that was not entirely under his control.'

'Come on now, Boss,' the healer's minders chipped in good naturedly, before the tortured, cured soul nervously revealed herself to the shaman, 'with all these people so tight around you, it would make more sense to ask who isn't touching you!'

'Friend,' he addressed her directly, 'your trust in me has made you well again. Don't worry. Everything's going to be alright.'

It is the one place in the Gospel accounts where we find Jesus in a magical milieu, from which, not only does he not recoil, but seems to embrace it without any word of disapproval, and in that embrace to elevate it to a different level of belief. He overlaid superstition with an ameliorating experience of unconditional acceptance.

She, aware of being ritually 'unclean', socially separate, had feared her touch had made him 'unclean' too, because that's what it said in the Law. Instead, by taking her 'uncleanness' into himself, he had not only made her 'clean', but had overturned a centuries old convention that was patriarchal in its origins. Her liberation was a sign of the intended liberation of all enslaved women. His knowledge and experience of transcendent reality outside himself met her interior and subjective spirituality without qualification, and the result had been dramatic.

It's an incident that contains clues for negotiating a creative convergence between the traditions of the great faiths and the new spiritual awareness that is occulture, in particular by means of the power of the imaginal.

While imagination is associated with ideas and the intellect, imaginal is to do with images, with the view we have of ourselves and others, with the pictures that inhabit our minds and that shape our souls.

An Imaginal World

Ezekiel was a uniquely imaginal person. His prophecies were almost exclusively shaped by the images created in his head when he was in one of his 'trances'.

> Under the wings of the cherubim there could be seen what looked like a human hand. I saw four wheels beside the cherubim, one wheel besides each cherub... I could hear the whirring of the wheels... When they moved, the wheels moved beside them... They spread their wings and raised themselves from the ground; I watched them go with the wheels beside them.

In terms of faith, the imaginal shifts the emphasis from the head to the heart, from the intellect to feelings, from the left side of the brain to the right. It acknowledges the emotional impact of our experiences and needs in assessing awareness of the Divine, and of the potential for the divine in our neighbor. It was what happened between Jesus and the unknown woman in the crowd. The image of her need countermanded the intellectual caveats of the law.

It is the recognition of the importance of the imaginal in religious awareness which accounts for the phenomenal success of Celtic spirituality. It may sometimes straddle the sentimental and the sensational, but at its sinewy best, it is disturbingly insightful.

Among the most loved and respected exponents of this kind of spirituality is the late John O'Donohue, Irish poet and scholar, whose book, *anam cara* ('soul friend'), is devoured equally by the newly spiritually aware as by those whose awareness is longer and within a faith tradition.

O'Donohue draws on spiritual wisdom from the Celtic world

to re-introduce us to a God we had forgotten, or perhaps had never met. He writes:

> In the Bible, it says that no one can see God and live. In a transferred sense, no one can see himself and live. All you can ever achieve is a sense of your soul. You gain little glimpses of its light, colors and contours. You feel the inspiration of its possibilities and the wonder of its mysteries.

The Christian expression that Jesus is the human face of God, or that Mary, his mother, was the Mother of God, is playing with similar ideas, using image as a window into the essential nature of 'Godness', and as a pattern and picture of human potential.

In the Celtic tradition, O'Donohue recalls, 'there is a fascinating interflow between soul and matter, between time and eternity':

> Between us the lost years insist on dreams
> That stir like crows among invisible ruins
> Disturbed by relics of laughter left in rooms
> Long after weather broke in where we had been.

When one of the world's leading theologians, Tubingen University's Jurgen Moltmann, proffers an endorsement of Celtic Spirituality, it is all the more noteworthy because it comes from the home of rigorous German scholarship. In a conference hosted by St Paul's Theological center and St Mellitus College at Holy Trinity, Brompton, in 2010, Moltmann described Celtic Spirituality as one of 'seeing the indwelling of God in all forms of life, so that we have to take all things into our reverence for life... It's a new cosmic form of spirituality, not a world-denying transcendent type of spirituality we are discovering today.'

I am not naturally an imaginal person, so I have never been allowed to forget the day I expressed my joy that the roses outside our front door were now in bloom, only to be told they'd been out for a couple of weeks! I had just not 'seen' them before. With time, the imaginal is becoming more important for me, helping me realize that without it the imagination can flounder.

The Chromosomes of God

The incident of the unknown woman in the crowd points to another difficulty in bridging the psychological gulf between magic and mystery. It concerns the gender imbalance that is subtly implicit in the perception and interpretation of mystery and magic, of seeing mystery as inherently masculine and magic as intrinsically feminine. It is an imbalance that continues to affect most societies, and is one in which the great monotheistic faiths have found almost seismic difficulties in living up to. That both genders are equally images of the divine was affirmed in the creation story in Genesis, chapter one:

> God created human beings in his own image;
> in the image of God he created them;
> male and female he created them.

There was, however, another version circulating in the collective memory in which Adam is the original creation and Eve is virtually an afterthought on God's part, put together from the man's spare bits! 'The rib he had taken out of the man the Lord God built her up into a woman...'

There was, nevertheless, a history of women in leadership and of women managing and organizing men. The so-called judges, that the tribal leaders called forth in times of crises to rally resistance to particular external threats, could be of either sex. So Judge Deborah takes her place in the pantheon of their past heroes and heroines to be celebrated in poetry and song for evermore:

Champions there were none,
none left in Israel,
until you, Deborah, arose,
arose as a mother in Israel.

It wasn't until the representational Queen Esther, in the book of Daniel, that another Jewish woman appears in a leadership role in Hebrew history, and then only as the concubine of a Persian monarch.

The Roman Catholic priest and social psychologist, Diarmuid O'Murchu, argues that we need to go even further back than Deborah, into so called 'deep time', where, in paleoanthropology, in the scientific study of human fossils, there is evidence, not only of greater equality between the sexes, but even of original female primacy. He is critical, therefore, of the tendency in the monotheistic faiths to confine their thinking to the comparatively limited time scale of their own histories, rather than taking in the much broader sweep of time, back to when the human animal first emerged from the primordial mud.

The question O'Murchu will not allow us to avoid is the relationship the Judean, Christian, Muslim God must have had with our human ancestors. In his book, *Ancestral Grace*, he writes:

Our great mistake today is to judge our entire story by the standard of the past eight thousand years. Intellectually and spiritually we have been conditioned into thinking small. The figure of two thousand years has taken on an archetypal significance never intended by God. It is easier to exert control when we keep things small, and the control is powerfully enhanced when we can religiously validate the context...

In all probability our ancestors were not into the tasks of

conquering and controlling that have become endemic to our patriarchal culture. They were certainly not passive, nor were they the helpless victims of ignorance and savagery. While not educated like us moderns, they were blessed with a wisdom that we have largely lost.

The unknown woman in the crowd, therefore, becomes a type common in most religious systems, and by derivation the societies that have shaped, and been shaped by, their outlook, of an inability to handle gender equality. The woman is socially compromised as a result of something today we would recognize as an easily treatable gynecological condition. Like many of her sex still, her condition had been used to forfeit her right to a distinct identity, so she remains anonymous throughout, and her credentials are further impugned by the primitiveness of her spirituality.

That similar attitudes still persist in so many societies, often with the connivance of the great faiths, under the cover of a narrow patriarchal theology, is a cause for continuing concern. 'Throughout the world at the present day,' Oxford historian, Diarmaid MacCulloch reminds us, 'the most easily heard tone in religion (not just Christianity) is a generally angry conservatism.' And it 'centers on a profound shift in gender roles which have traditionally been given religious significance and validated by religious tradition.'

The church fathers, from Tertullian to Clement of Alexandria, were far too prone to draw out the lessons of the Garden of Eden as evidence for an inherent weakness in women, rather than as an illustration of the unisex nature of temptation.

The twentieth century poet, Gwenallt, in Emyr Huphreys' adaptation of his poem on *The Serpent*, provides a more balanced picture of what Eden was all about, homing in on the snake and pinpointing Adam's equal culpability!

Like ivy climbing you wrapped your cunning about
The tender bark of the forbidden tree
Luring into its shade the naked lout
To sow the seed of Death in Arcady.

Within the Christian tradition, both the Roman Catholic and the Orthodox churches still persist in ruling out the priesthood of women on the grounds that priesthood and maleness are indivisible. Some evangelical churches can be equally adamant that authority in the church is the sole prerogative and responsibility of men. Meanwhile, the worldwide Anglican Communion is straining at the leash to remain united, with Provinces that can and do welcome and affirm the priesthood of women, and their eligibility to be nominated to be bishops. The Jewish rabbinate has the same division of understanding and tension within its ranks. There are even a few rare voices in Islam that are now challenging the assertion that Imams and Sheikhs can only be men, arguing that there is no evidence in the Qur'an that this is anything other than a cultural custom.

When a black woman decides to make a pot
The clay wet and white on her dry hands,
the Anglican priest, Flora Winfield, whispers in our ear:
Shaping the soft clay between them
Jeremiah's God's daughter
Remakes the world.

Even when the traditionalists within the great monotheistic faiths extol the preciousness of women, and vie with each other to laud women's unique place within creation, the effect is only to re-enforce male dominance, and male control over women. Moreover, because of the closeness of religious attitudes to the societies in which they exert influence, even in those societies that may be largely secular, the subordination of women becomes an issue of much wider consequence than simply one of internal religious ideology.

In a survey in the year 2000 CE, by an Edinburgh-based initiative to change attitudes regarding violence against women, it emerged that, 'some girls still thought it acceptable for a male to hit them if she "deserved" it'! And a similar enquiry in Wales around the same time uncovered shocking tales of failures by faith institutions not only to protect women from domestic violence, but also to condemn the stunted theology that gave it a spurious legitimacy.

So the magical and the feminine have been fused together to suggest all those elements that are viewed with suspicion and that need controlling, to the detriment of healthy maleness and healthy femaleness. When the healer in the Gospel story, as the incarnate presence of the mystery of God, affirmed the unknown woman in the crowd, he broke through social conventions, as well as religious taboos, for all time.

Watering the Middle Ground

If these rivers of magic and mystery continue to be thought of as running in opposite directions, not just at different speeds, to swirl and spin, to whirl and reel on endlessly, they will create an island of ignorance where people will live in suspicion and fear of each other, rather than watering the middle ground to make it fecund and fertile.

Magic challenges the monotheistic faiths to acknowledge that people have different ways of tapping into the divine. In their turn, the Faiths challenge the world of occulture to face the costly side of spirituality.

The 'Eucatastrophe'

In his seminal 1939 Andrew Lang Essay, 'On Fairy Stories', Tolkien presents the ultimate resolution of difference as the moment of 'eucatastrophe'. The 'sudden joyous turn' at the climax of a story, is less the simplistic 'happy after' conclusion, but rather the tale's 'redemptive morality'. Thus (in a perceptive but unattributed entry on the internet), the ending of Tolkien's *The Lord of the Rings* is 'not entirely "happy".'

> Frodo is forever scarred and broken by his quest and struggle with the power of the Ring. The elves are leaving Middle-earth ... so are Bilbo, Frodo, and Gandalf.
>
> The true 'eucatastrophe' of the novel is not the 'happily ever after' but the downfall of Sauron and Gollum's role as the destroyer of the Ring. Sauron's fall came about because of his attempts at domination, which led him to invest his power in a single object (the Ring). Gollum, whose fatal flaw was his lust for the Ring, contributed directly to its destruction.
>
> Frodo and Samwise succeed because of both their unselfish bravery (undertaking the quest to Mt Doom) and their pity (in sparing Gollum). These ideas, while beneath the surface of the writing, were central to Tolkien's themes. This was Tolkien's 'eucatastrophe', a sort of 'poetic justice' and redemption that Tolkien believed was essential to a fairy-story.

It engages our attention and stimulates our imagination because it also rings true to ordinary life. Resolution is a costly business and it is seldom as clear cut or as neat as we might wish or imagine.

Our Lady of Penrhys

When the windswept estate of Penrhys, one of the largest social housing projects in Wales, decided to hold a festival to mark forty years of its existence, a 'fairy tale' ending looked far from assured. Perched on a mountaintop between the two Rhondda valleys, the community was anxious to redress its reputation which had become synonymous with decay and social breakdown.

Providing the estate with some sense of an older history was a nearby medieval shrine to Mary, which was still the object of Christian devotion and pilgrimage. In its day, Our Lady of Penrhys had been as famous as Our Lady of Walsingham, and the estate's ecumenical church (Anglican combined with seven Free Church traditions) had been named 'Llanfair' ('St Mary's Church'), with the Abbot of Caldey preaching at its opening,

By a strange coincidence, the date for the estate's celebration happened to be the day before the wider Catholic community would be marking the 470th anniversary of the shrine's desecration at the hands of Henry VIII.

All seemed set for an inspirational month-long 'Pilgrims' Festival' that would bring together the old and the new, the secular and the sacred, coming to a climax in a kind of joyous 'eucatastrophe'. The potential of the occasion, therefore, created a lot of excitement. But it also exposed a lot of confusion and angst! Some suspected the proposed Festival of having a paganizing agenda. Some baulked at an act of Marian devotion verging on the exclusive. Misunderstandings abounded. But there were also genuine differences to be recognized and appreciated.

Thanks partly to the intervention of a Catholic, who stressed the potential of the shrine as a means of healing and wholeness, not only for the community but beyond, a way ahead was gradually hammered out. Angela drew on her experience as a writer and broadcaster to help devise a Christian act of worship for the Sunday, which not only honored the sensibilities of her own tradition, but opened up the event so that all the community's different faith traditions were included and heard equally. During the service, residents too expressed in their own terms what this 'holy place' had come to mean for them.

In the end, everyone who regarded the mountain top as

special found out a little more about each other, including Pagans and New Agers and those with no label, and the secularist and the atheists and the indifferent. And on the day of the service, even the 'hard men' of the community came and listened from behind the wall!

Angela felt the ground was better-prepared, therefore, for respectful and serious dialogue and collaboration with the wider constituency of people for whom the site was special. Writing about it afterwards, she noted that while Catholics were becoming increasingly open to doing things together with other Christian Churches, and more open to doing some things with the other great Religions of the world, the dialogue with contemporary culture, 'with those who believe in the spiritual life but not in "religion"', was still viewed with suspicion and reservation.

In the attempt to understand where our contemporaries are, she also found herself having to engage with that other issue of importance: Enchantment.

The theory goes (to summarize it crudely) that aspects of the Reformation, the Enlightenment, Romanticism and Modernism have dis-enchanted the world. It used to be full of numinous presences. The sacred was everywhere. But rationality and individualism dis-enchanted us. The gods, and even God, departed, or were chased away. But there is a school of thought which posits that the world is becoming Re-enchanted and the evidence can be found in the increasing interest in the spiritual so that it is possible to argue that society may be experiencing sacralization rather than secularization.

Jesus may have commanded his followers to love their neighbors, but, as Angela pointed out, our neighbors today, certainly in Britain and Ireland, 'are mostly not in organized religion but in the maze of "alternative" spiritualities and lifestyles that are one of the signs of our times.'

*

The Babylonian priest, Sughurim was curious about the religion of the recent exiles from the West, and went out of his way to befriend them, to find out more about their customs and their practices, their country and their God. He felt he'd found a kindred spirit in the young priest, Ezekiel, though the Hebrew was never as forthcoming as he would have liked. There was always a sense of reserve, even when they'd got to know each other: a holding back; a sense of spiritual superiority that was, if he was honest, quite irritating.

So their conversations were invariably stilted, even formal. Sughurim, despite appearances, was convinced that the Hebrew was not as antagonistic as he sometimes sounded when he was railing against the Philistines and the Edomites, the Egyptians and the Tyrenians.

'Your god,' Sughurim ventured when he'd got to know the Hebrew better, 'he didn't look after you all that well, did he?'

'Not so,' Ezekiel shot back. 'We let him down. We failed him. We didn't abide by his commandments.'

'Our Marduk is satisfied if we just keep offering him sacrifices. He doesn't require anything more of us. But he guarantees our victories.'

Ezekiel looked up, a mixture of pity and disbelief on his face. 'How can Marduk guarantee anything? He's just an elaborate statue. A piece of painted stone. An inanimate block!'

And that's how their conversations usually ended, with neither able to get into the mind of the other, both equally baffled by each other's intransigence.

It was Ezekiel's certainty that got under Sughurim's skin, his conviction that their God would one day gather them together again and lead them back to their pathetic little country, 'to prove his holiness in the sight of the nations'! How long would it take them to realise, Sughurim wondered, that they were settled in Babylon for good; that this was their future, and their children's future; that Babylon would last a thousand years and more?

Let the dry land appear

5. Between Merciless and Merciful

We strain to glimpse your mercy-seat
and find you kneeling at our feet
Brian Wren

The Jacob Epstein sculpture of Christ in Majesty in the Cathedral Church of Saint Peter and Saint Paul in Llandaf does not so much look down on the congregation, as to gaze beyond it. Pinned to his obtrusive concrete arch, but freed of his deadly cross, this Jewish Christ is not so much indifferent, as slightly removed from the comings and goings below.

Along the nave, embroidered priests process purposefully, while in the chancel white-wrapped choristers prepare to vie with Cherubim and Seraphim for the attention of the church of Dyfrig, Teilo and Euddogrwydd beyond the veil, as well as the one here and now. Organ pedal, swell and great stops announce that the liturgy is about to begin, calling the quick and the dead to witness, once again, the never-ending Eucharist. And the faithful repeat: 'Lord, have mercy. Christ, have mercy'.

But the aluminum figure above them, his hands healed of their wounds, his feet restored, appears not to be listening, as in their Sunday-bests the people plead with God to 'Have mercy upon us. Most merciful Father'. The Dean, resplendent in voice and vestments, prays for sovereign, bishop and ordinary folk, and the polite congregation responds contritely, 'Lord in thy mercy'.

Called to the altar, where wafer and wine have become a taster for the heavenly feast to come, the suppliants diffidently protest, 'We do not presume to come to this Thy table, O merciful Lord'. And confronted by the enormity of what's being done, and has been done, for them and for all, by the figure above and beyond them, they again entreat the Lamb of God, 'who takes away the sins of the world' to 'have mercy upon us'.

And when it's all over, and they pick up their hymn books with their coats and umbrellas, and take their leave of Epstein's Christ and the weekly liturgy, they muse as they go, 'For his mercy endures forever'. In the Reformed churches and chapels nearby, where they sing their hymns with gusto, their voices are also raised in proclamation of 'a wideness in God's mercy, like the wideness of the sea'; and in sober anticipation of communion, to offer thanksgiving for the 'Bread of the world in mercy broken'.

While, to the west, in Cyncoed Gardens, in the ultra-modern United Synagogue in Cardiff's salubrious suburbs, the staunch but diminishing Jewish community gather on Shabbat to worship Ezekiel's God, and to hear the cantor intone in an ever-present timelessness, 'Have mercy on me, O Lord, for I am withered away'.

Nearer the city center, some of Cardiff's eleven thousand Muslims meet for Friday prayers in Britain's first mosque to meet the spiritual needs of the newly settled Yemeni sailors. Renamed the Al-Manar Islamic center, its unshod congregation, in serried ranks on its well-worn carpeted floor, kneels in submission 'in the name of Allah the all Merciful, the most compassionate'.

For large swathes of believers in Cathedrals, churches and chapels, in Synagogues and Mosques, over countless centuries, the mercy of God has expressed a theological insight, as well as shaping a liturgical response. It has articulated the generosity of God alongside an acknowledgement of human unworthiness. At its best it is, and always has been, the idea of our being loved despite ourselves!

Within those faiths, however, there are those for whom

mercy seems somehow unworthy, even wrong, to describe who and what they mean by God. For yet others, who have moved away from the faiths in which they grew up, the continuing usage of mercy to celebrate and interpret the mysteries of spirituality only reaffirms their conviction that they no longer belong within the old religious frameworks.

Mercy can be a problem, therefore, for many conventional believers, as well as for those who have chosen to nurture their spirituality in different soil. For both of them, mercy is one of those concepts whose meaning relies on what it might be like without it! Always in the background of mercy they see the hovering shadow of the merciless. For them, the merciful are lauded because of what they are not, and it is that negative that gets in the way of their seeing mercy as a good word for God.

How, then, are we to feel our way between these twin reactions to mercy, the one positive, the other negative, so that the appreciation of each may be refined by a better understanding of the other: between those who draw on invocations of 'Lord, have mercy', for daily comfort and strength, and those who shudder at the very thought?

Tit-for-Tat Justice

Definitions of mercy vary, but all include the idea of 'compassion or forgiveness shown towards a person in one's power.' For the liturgical conscientious objectors, it is the 'in one's power' that gets in the way of accepting mercy as a commendation for a God they have come to experience as approachable and accepting. Their intention is not to deny the cost of acceptance, but they regard power as an awkward component in an otherwise affirming relationship. Even the usage of mercy in such compassionate contexts as 'mercy killing', referring to the terminating of the life of someone suffering from an incurable disease, does not compensate sufficiently for all those other times where its absence has been bewailed.

The King Zedekiahs of this world (Zedekiah, the vassal imposed by Babylon after King Jehoiachin had been taken away into exile), may have pleaded for mercy when he was captured after his ill-judged uprising, but it didn't save him from suffering the same fate as their national folk hero, Samson:

> Betrayed, captived, and both my eyes put out,
> Made of my enemies the scorn and gaze,
> To grind in brazen fetters under task...

Even the beatitude: 'Blessed are those who show mercy; mercy shall be shown them', is no more than a well-meaning injunction that relies on good will and fair play. A victor's justice is summary: a victor's mercy unqualified. The pleas for mercy from martyrs and hostages alike deface the pages of history, and sear the noblest enterprises of those nations. Whether the powerful exercise or withhold mercy is, therefore, beside the point. What matters is that they could.

It is this connection that objectors to mercy, as an attribute of God, find so unsatisfactory. They cannot conceive of a Supreme Being to whose better nature they have to appeal if they're to avoid destruction in this world and eternal torment in the next. The issue is not that God is merciful, but that even by thinking of God in those terms, there is the lingering doubt that behind a temporary reprieve there lurks a nasty, vindictive, malevolent Deity!

The Canadian author, Margaret Atwood, did a similar piece of debunking on the portrayal of Portia in Shakespeare's *Merchant of Venice*. Behind her honeyed words about the quality of mercy:

> It droppeth as the gentle rain from heaven
> Upon the place beneath: it is twice blest;
> It blesseth him that gives and him that takes...

the thrust of Portia's courtroom performance is that Shylock needs to be 'more merciful than everyone else has been to him. When Shylock can't manage this, Portia reverts to eye-for-an-eye tit-for-tat justice and more'!

An over-emphasis on mercy can lead to a perversion of wholesome religion, and in the Christian faith has produced a doctrine claiming that God's wrath upon the whole of humankind, for its willful sinfulness, was only averted because Jesus stepped in and, without the benefits of mercy, bore the brunt of it. Such a theology is morally objectionable as well as theologically suspect, and every time God is saddled with the term 'mercy' or 'merciful' there is the danger of the distortion being perpetuated. Even 'the Jesus prayer' that became such a refreshing means of a praying together for people of different faiths (referred to in chapter three), is open to the same charge with its repeated call for divine mercy. The danger lies in seeming to give God a bad name, and it is done, however innocently and unintentionally, every time the devout invoke the Lord to 'have mercy', or to address Allah as 'all merciful'.

God Never Changes His Mind

In its defense, it may be argued that as the currency of faith, 'mercy' is an unevenly balanced transaction between God and humankind. One side gets more than it deserves; the other gives more than it is obliged to. Mercy thus breaks the contract in favor of the debtor. That, however, is not how mercy is perceived by those outside the circle of this kind of thinking. In the world of tabloid headlines, too often 'mercy' relates to situations where mercy has been tragically missing, where mercy has too often been in very short supply, with babies tortured, women and girls abused, and children conscripted to kill 'without mercy'.

In the home where relationships can be volatile and the children live in fear of the temper of the elders entrusted with their care, mercy is a poor substitute for love. Those with such experiences can, moreover, find the very word 'father', and sometimes 'mother', evoking deeply negative thoughts, conjuring up memories of unpredictability, abuse and violence.

When Jesus addressed God as 'Daddy/Abba', he was breaking a taboo that had cast God for too long as unapproachable and unpredictable. When the whole world seemed to be closing in on him and it seemed as if he still had the option of avoiding a final confrontation with the fate that awaited him, if he escaped while there was still time, while it was still dark, it is with Abba/Daddy that Jesus pleaded in the Garden of Gethsemane, not with some strict, implacable Deity.

At his most spiritually sensitive, Ezekiel has some astoundingly affectionate and endearing images of a God, comparing his people in one exceptionally beautiful passage, to a foundling adopted by a Generous Stranger:

I tended you like an evergreen plant growing in the fields; you throve and grew. You came to full womanhood... I came by and saw that you were ripe for love. I spread the skirt of my robe over you and covered your naked body. I plighted my troth and entered into a covenant with you, says the Lord God, and you became mine... you became a great beauty and rose to be a queen. Your beauty was famed throughout the world, it was perfect because of the splendor I bestowed on you.

Drawing on such imagery, Christianity has gone on to make even more daring claims for the potential of his divine/human relationship. In a remarkable sermon on forgiveness, the late Herbert McCabe, a Dominican priest, startled his congregation with this sobering assessment:

Never be deluded into thinking that if you have contrition, if you are sorry for your sins, God will come and forgive you, that he will be touched by your appeal, change his mind about you and forgive you. Not a bit of it. God never changes his mind about you. He is simply in love with you. What he does again and again is change your mind about him. That is why you are sorry. That is what forgiveness is. You are not forgiven because you confess your sin. You confess your sin, recognize yourself for what you are, because you are forgiven.

Nothing, therefore, could be further from that insidious notion of a suspended sentence on account of the mercy of an all powerful Deity, or because the Cross allowed the declaration of a once and for all amnesty for condemned sinners!

Religious people need to get their heads around the usage of omnipotence in relation to God. Philosophers may be able to argue (quite properly) that God's omnipotence and human freedom are not incompatible, but most are not philosophers and it is better to think of power in relation to God as the power of love. Love is the dry land between waters that can threaten to drown us.

In a spirited exchange between Jesus and the disciple Peter, it had been Peter's intention to get Jesus to adjudicate once and for all on the acceptable limits of forgiveness, but it went horribly wrong! Perhaps his brother, Andrew, had got on his nerves one time too many, taking advantage of kinship rather than showing kindness; or those terrible twins, James and John, had elbowed him out of the way once too often, with that air of superiority he found so grating. Or Judas had asked him for another loan, when Peter's purse was already full of Judas' unredeemed IOUs.

Whatever the cause, Peter's capacity for forgiveness was exhausted. It was time to establish some ground rules. 'Leader, if a friend causes me pain over and over again,' he complained, 'how many times must I let it go?' He'd thought of suggesting three, but decided to double it, to appear in a good light. At the last minute, however, he thought he'd better it by going for seven. Jesus seemed to like seven. He'd told stories about seven evil spirits and about seven brothers, and he'd been impressed by that lad who'd shared his seven loaves with them. There was that woman from Magdala, too, who Jesus said had seven devils, and he'd exorcised all of them. And in seven days God had called the world into existence. He'd go for seven.

Jesus' response had quite thrown him off balance. He'd been expecting to be singled out for his exceptional forbearance; to put the others to shame, to be top disciple for once. Not a bit of it. 'Not seven times,' Jesus replied. 'Seventy times seven would be nearer the mark.' Peter retired to lick his wounds. Jesus could be quite inscrutable at times!

Seventy times seven is Bible-speak for unqualified, immeasurable. It is limitless forgiveness. No conditions. It's everybody's for the taking. Mercy, on the other hand, is the currency of justice. There's a necessary place for that in an imperfect world between individuals in community. But forgiveness is a different coinage altogether. It doesn't negate justice; it supersedes it. It's not based on retribution; it works by absorbing it. Forgiveness is the currency of love.

'The Sacred Presence in Things'

For those for whom mercy means being merciful, mercy is, of course, a very good way to live. It is about feeding the hungry, giving drink to the thirsty, clothing the naked, welcoming the stranger, visiting the sick, befriending the prisoner, and giving the dead an honorable burial. The members of various religious orders engaged in nursing or similar work are, therefore, rightly known and admired as 'Sisters of Mercy'.

On the other hand, for those for whom there is some ambivalence about mercy, it can be a bad way to live if it leads to an undermining of personal responsibility. On this reading, it can be argued that it doesn't matter what we do, or don't do, because in the end, whether we live or die, depends on an arbitrary divine 'thumbs-up', or a 'thumbs-down' in the arena of human existence. Since, therefore, our theology influences our lifestyle and our outlook much more than we are sometimes prepared to acknowledge, the theology of mercy can be open to frustrating the very good it is supposed to promote. The way we see the world matters.

In 2009, the Prince of Wales used his invitation to deliver the BBC's Dimbleby Lecture to regret the current trend to neglect philosophy and religion in any meaningful analysis of how we perceive the world. Discussion in the public square seems to be wholly dominated by a mechanistic 'what works' attitude, with very little discourse on what things mean, and of what he called 'the sacred presence in things.' In view of his widely attested interest in faith issues, it was not an unexpected intervention, but the Prince's description of religion as concerned with 'the sacred presence in things' surely merits further reflection.

The argument of a mature spirituality is knowing that we are loved and this makes us aware of 'the sacred presence in things', which, in turn, restores a sense of responsibility towards our world, towards others and ourselves. Without that, we become careless and selfish, thoughtless and profligate, arrogant and irresponsible. We become unlovable, because we cannot really love anyone or anything. God loved Ezekiel's people. It would take further theological awareness in subsequent generations to see that what was true for them was true for all human kind. This is not a narrow, nationalistic, exclusive love. God is too big for that sort of nonsense. God doesn't love selectively or in self-contained packages. It's a cornucopia of love, pressed and shaken down and running over, overflowing love.

It was Ezekiel's refusal to give up on that conviction, however imperfectly grasped, however ethno-centric in its perception, that saved them. Because to be loved, is to release love. To be loved is to be accepted without qualification: no ifs, no buts.

This is the missing element in much of contemporary Western society. It lies behind the breakdown of the family unit, the loss of community, the fear of immigrants and the widening of the gap between the poor and the well off. In our frightening self confidence, we have lost the capacity to accept our own vulnerability. We're afraid to admit that we've made mistakes and might be wrong, because we have no system for appropriating forgiveness. We need to feel the Friar Preacher, Herbert McCabe, tap on our shoulder to tell us that, 'It's OK, you can admit the truth about yourself. It doesn't matter: God loves you anyway.'

The Abrahamic faiths may share a common story in their witness that 'God is a rock; God is One; God is good; God exists', as Karen Armstrong puts it pithily in her book, *The Case for God: What Religion Really Means*, but they differ in their emphasises, sometimes quite significantly. Christianity's take on God, despite the liturgical undertow that might suggest otherwise, is that mercy is dated, redundant, obsolete. The compassionate response of love to love, underestimated or misunderstood, is quite a different currency to mercy.

*

Was it because he knew himself to be loved by Tamar that Ezekiel was able to contemplate the depth of a Divine love as constant, as true?

Hannah, their nearest neighbor in Tel-abib, had been worried about Ezekiel's wife, Tamar. Hannah felt sure that he couldn't be the easiest man to live with, not that her Reuben was much of a catch! What Hannah called Ezekiel's 'street theatre', all that lying about, now on one side, now on another, for weeks on end, just wasn't natural in her book. She had tried to get Tamar to see her point of view, to get Ezekiel to behave more normally, like other priests; to not make such a spectacle of himself all the time. But Tamar would never speak a word against the man she called 'her handsome apple tree', 'her gorgeous gazelle'.

'He does take some understanding,' was the most Tamar would ever admit. 'He does what he does because he has to, because he believes it. Because it's what he says God's told him to do: to be our people's "watchman".'

I have appointed you, O man, a watchman for the Israelites, and you must pass to them any warnings you receive from me.

When memories were wrapped in fables, they said that under the sea in Cardigan Bay there was a lost city, *Cantre'r Gwaelod*, drowned when the drunken watchman, Seithenyn, abandoned his post and left the floodgates open. They say you can still hear the bells of that sunken city tolling when the wind is set fair, warning of imminent danger ignored. Watchmen can never afford to drop their guard.

'I'm sure he's sincere, everyone knows that,' Hannah came back, 'but does he ever think of the effect it's having on you, and on the children. What do they think of their dad when he carries on in public, the way he does?'

'It can be difficult, I'll grant you that,' Tamar admitted, 'especially when he refused to say a word, even to me or the kids, for days on end, but once he'd seen it though, he was a delight to be with again, telling me my cheeks were lovely between my plaited tresses, and my eyes like doves behind my veil!' She blushed at the remembrance of it.

Hannah envied the relationship Tamar and Ezekiel had. She knew how he doted on her. And she too seemed so happy with him, for all his oddities. She only wished Reuben could be a bit more like Ezekiel sometimes!

*

The 'sacred presence in things' might not have been part of the religious language of Ezekiel, but the idea was certainly integral to the thinking of this most spiritual of all the Hebrew prophets. When he opened his heart to the elite of the exiles, his concern was less with why things were the way they were, rather than in what they meant.

They would meet in his house, sit in his courtyard, hear his ideas, argue over why this national calamity had befallen them, testing the very foundations of their belief system. They would wonder aloud whether it was time to let go of all that Hebrew religion, that Temple orientated worship, and adopt the new creeds of Babylon that promised power and influence and prosperity. They were tired of beating their breasts over what had gone wrong. Hashem or Marduk – did it matter?

Ezekiel, though, refused to be deflected, and worried at 'the sacred presence in things'; he worried so intensely at times that it seemed to transfix, transform and transfigure him as if he was in another world, seeing an alternative reality, voicing words that resonated with something authentic, disturbing but also quite radical in their memory and experience.

The Scapegoat Flaw

The theology underlining mercy in the context of a transaction finds its origins in the concept of the scapegoat: 'a person who is blamed for the wrongdoings or mistakes of others', after the Hebrew practice of 'a goat sent into the wilderness after the Jewish chief priest had symbolically laid the sins of the people upon it'.

In Leviticus, the third book of the Torah, Moses had instructed his brother, Aaron, 'to bring forward a live goat' into the Tent of Meeting, where the people were assembled for the annual rite of public atonement. 'Laying both his hands on its head', Aaron 'must confess over it all the iniquities of the Israelites and all their acts of rebellion, that is all their sins; he is to lay his hands on the head of the goat and send it away into the wilderness in the charge of a man who is waiting ready. The goat will carry all their iniquities upon itself into some barren waste, where the man will release it, there in the wilderness'.

It is a powerful liturgy for giving expression in an unforgettable way to the seriousness of individual and corporate wrongdoing. It is affirming the need for bad actions arising from systemic social failure to be recognized as such, and cleansed from the body politic. The Truth and Reconciliation Commissions, that originated in post-apartheid South Africa to handle the burden of past wrongs (since taken up in many other countries seeking to come to terms with collective trauma), are a refinement of the scapegoat directive. It resonates with Christian understanding of there being no healing of memories without the admission that what was done, whatever the motive, inflicted corporate as well as individual pain and that unless it is faced up to, it will fester and undermine future development.

Even the Suffering Servant imagery of the prophet Isaiah, which has so enriched Christian theology, can be misunderstood if, instead of endorsing the concept of unqualified love in response to human wickedness and its consequences (in war, pain and suffering; cruelty, greed and violence), it appears to portray a schizophrenic God: on the one hand, an all-loving God, and on the other, a God to whom humanity's 'pound of flesh' is due.

A better interpretation, which doesn't deny justice or gloss over human responsibility, is that which affirms that when one suffers for all, and that one is innocent, it is not to assuage the need for Divine vengeance, but an act of Divine love. The enormity of the wrongdoing is embraced by the enormity of the love.

There is no more powerful image than that of the Crucified God, captured in great art and sculpture from Michelangelo to Epstein, from Carravagio to Graham Sutherland: the dying God that can seem so perplexing to other religions, which otherwise share so much with Christianity. Yet, its very shockingness is its strength. It's a supreme act of human love meeting a supreme act of Divine love. It is not the child meeting the parent's demand for retribution, but the parent's love dying in the place of, and for, and in the child.

For the Italian Christian Chiara Lubich, who founded the Focolare movement in the aftermath of the Second World War, costly discipleship is the consequence of costly love. Focolare has since become an international ecumenical phenomenon committed to putting unity into practice, between peoples, between God and humanity, between the religions, and with those of no religion. In her book, *The Cry*, written towards the end of her long life, she sees the love of God most completely captured in that awful cry of dereliction from the cross, when Jesus appropriates to himself the words of the psalm: 'My God, my God, why hast thou forsaken me?'

'It is a *real* abandonment for his divinity,' she says, 'because Jesus being God is one with the Father and with the Holy Spirit, and cannot be separated: at most he can be distinct. But this distinction is not pain: it is love.' She quotes the Orthodox Ecumenical Patriarch, Bartholomew of Constantinople's insight that: 'The abyss of despair vanishes, like an insignificant drop of hatred in an infinite abyss of love. The distance between the Father and the Son is no longer the place of hell, but of the Spirit.'

Those recoiling from, or even uneasy with, pleas for God's mercy may, therefore, quietly offer instead: 'Lord, you love us; Lord, you love us; Lord, you love us', recognizing that after centuries and millennia of usage in synagogues, cathedrals and mosques, it is well nigh impossible to conceive of an alternative liturgical refrain now replacing: 'Lord have mercy'.

Let its usage, though, carry at least a hint of unease! And let its users be aware that every time they tie the label 'mercy' around God's neck, they should be doing so with considerable reservation!

Brian Wren, one of the most gifted of later twentieth century hymnists, was always on the lookout for better language to express in song what is to be believed. As we try to feel our way to a theology, caught between the positive and negative of mercy, it is hard to better his phrasing in his hymn, 'Great God, your love has called us here / as we, by love for love were made':

...not through some merit, right or claim
but by your gracious love alone.
We strain to glimpse your mercy-seat
and find you kneeling at our feet.

For Wren, it is God who kneels audaciously at our feet, not us at the feet of God. In its endeavor to hold justice and forgiveness together, mercy can miss the mark for many, because justice evaluates responsibility and pronounces punishment, and forgiveness seeks to absorb and absolve, to take the pain of wrongdoing into itself, and to draw its sting.

6. Between Heaven and Hell

he comes every night without fail.
Christine James

Nella Last was a housewife in Barrow-in-Furness who kept a diary recording her everyday thoughts during and immediately following the 1939/45 CE war. They were her contribution to a project run by the Mass Observation Archive, and might never have seen the light of day had not some enterprising researcher come upon them years later and released extracts, which became two bestselling books and, in 2006, a film for ITV with Victoria Wood in the title role. Nella writes as one imagines she spoke – directly.

'I don't believe in Heaven or Hell, in the resurrection of the body,' she admits in one of her entries, though, as her editors point out, 'she did, however, believe in a supernatural power. She seemed to hold the view that God was everywhere and in everything, and she sometimes spoke of a "Force" or "Plan" or "Rhythm" in life, as if she felt that humans were in some sense under the firm direction of a higher being... She also had a Hindu-like conviction that individual life continued after death. "I've always had a strong belief in life going on," she wrote on 28th February 1950, "not a Heaven where there is singing and walking by green pastures, but somewhere where we got the chances we threw away, or never had, to grow".'

It's a conviction that is probably common to more than might be willing to admit it, including churchgoing people.

One such person was Bella James, a highly regarded member of the congregation where I was once the minister. Bella, struggling with ill-health in her eighties, and reluctant to accept that her husband, Harry, a remarkably articulate physicist, had to be admitted to a care home after a second stroke deprived him of the power of movement and coherent speech, confided, 'I don't believe in heaven'.

Here was someone brought up in the Christian faith, a pillar in every local church to which she and her husband had belonged: someone who had thought about what she believed and what was believable, and who, with her husband, had nurtured a family in a Christian environment. She had also faced some of the big questions of faith, the greatest of which was the birth of their first child, a boy born with Spina Bifida, who died nine months later on Christmas Day.

Never a year went by that Bella didn't note his birth date, imagining his growing up, and what might have been. And at the back of her mind, the rumbling, unspoken, unanswered question – where was her first born now? Nor did she gain any comfort from hymns that speculated on

… a home for little children
Above the bright blue sky,
Where Jesus reigns in glory,
A home of peace and joy.

Faith leaders have to think about death more often than most. Are they whistling in the dark? Are they insulating numbed feelings from accepting the inevitability of our mortality? They conduct funerals. They repeat comfortable words. Are expressions of resurrection euphemisms for the continuity of life that we see in nature, or are they intimations of something else? And does it matter?

If it matters at all, it matters not in what it promises beyond, but in what it implies about how we live now. And the priests and the pastors, the rabbis and the imams, generally haven't always been very good at handling doubt while dispensing consolation. Alongside the comfortable words, they have not shown how the idea of heaven can be acknowledged, as and when one has outgrown the literalness of the imagery in sacred writings and inspired paintings.

Those stories and their artistic representations are beautiful in themselves and can be treasured as such, but they are also signs of something that defies description and can still be appreciated and appropriated once we learn how to read them with refined reasoning.

The great gift of a living spirituality is that it throws up interpreters who can help to bridge the credibility gap without losing the plot. It was part of the genius of Pope Gregory the Great, that when his missionary priests reported their inability to make inroads into Britain's native pagan roots, he advised them against destroying what they could not change. Rather, they should overlay the old with the new insights of the faith that was theirs, drawing out the latent, native truth in the shrines and groves, the burial places of the inhabitants of this rugged land.

Impossible to Put Into Language

The good souls who give up on a theology that includes heaven, because they cannot get their heads around the numbers, should be praised for challenging a literal-mindedness that fails to connect. Of course it's preposterous to think of all the six and a half billion people alive today, times all the descendants of our genetic Eve over the last two hundred millennia, as well as those as yet unborn, on our little planet, which is only one of a trillion in the universe, as living on forever in some alternative dimension, as matter and substance and form!

It is idle to expect descriptions of heaven formulated in the thought forms of their times, and attributed to the founders and exponents of the great faiths to be taken literally. When Jesus taught his disciples to pray, 'Our Father in heaven', it was sufficient that they had an understanding of God with, but also beyond, them. When Jesus was dying on the cross, and told one of the thieves crucified at his side, 'Today you will be with me in Paradise', it was an affirmation not only of the continuity of life, but of the place of self-awareness in realizing its possibilities.

When the Apostle Paul confessed in a letter to the small band of Corinthian believers that once, 'fourteen years before', he'd been 'so close to Jesus' that he'd found himself (like Ezekiel), 'transported beyond the world of time and space,' he roused the curiosity of generations to come into the nature and character of heaven! 'Whether it was real or my imagination,' Paul went on to say in the down to earth paraphrase of the *Good as New translation*, 'God only knows. I was in God's Garden, and I heard things it's impossible to put into human language.'

*

There seemed no reason why Tamar should have fallen ill – she of the lovely cheeks between her plaited tresses, the love of Ezekiel's life, with her eyes like doves behind her veil. She was as strong as she was beautiful. She had borne him a succession of healthy children. She was still so young. There were so many more years to look forward to, sharing her company and her laughter, wiping her tears, holding her tenderly, way into the old age of their three score years and ten. She needed to be there for him, for their children; he wanted her to be at his side when his prophecies would be vindicated and they'd be able to go home, back to Zion. It didn't make sense for Tamar to be so ill.

But her condition deteriorated rapidly. The children were called and Ezekiel seemed utterly destroyed as he clasped her hand as she was gathered into Abraham's bosom. The light of his life was gone. The fairest of women, his lily, snatched away, senselessly. Her sweet voice, not be heard again.

I spoke to the people in the morning. That evening my wife died.

He tried to deny the pain of it, to make sense of it. It was as if God was telling him:

...you are not to wail or weep or give way to tears. Suppress your grief, and observe no mourning for the dead. Wrap your turban on your head and put on your sandals You are not to veil your beard in mourning, or eat the bread of sorrow.

So he carried on much as normal. His feelings sublimated, bottled up, denied, but he could not conceal them completely; and once, just once, they slip past his guarded heart as he remembers that she was 'the dearest thing' he had ever known.

*

The American poet, Mary Lee, captures the poignancy of loss in these lines from 'In Between'. She recalls the daily telephone conversations between Pittsburgh and London that she used to have with her mother, sharing the trivialities (a broken watch, a missed bus) that bond a relationship:

In between the sentences,
In the gaps between words,
I heard her yearn towards me.

There'd been the annual meetings to look forward to, alternating between the States and the UK, and gratitude that her mother had lived long enough to hold her only grandson and to 'push him in his stroller' as she'd once pushed her. The sparseness of the words in her last stanza captures the awful loneliness that can accompany bereavement:

I speak to her
When I am alone,
Telling her the small things...
In between the sentences,
In the gaps between words,
I hear the broken place.

How Ezekiel coped with his 'broken place' has seemed unnatural by comparison, even callous to some, because he dealt with his pain by trying to see some hidden meaning in it, some clue that it might after all be part of some larger plan, and he convinced himself that it was so. He turned his tragedy into another of his parables to foretell the ruin that was to befall his people.

The people asked me what meaning my actions had for them.
I answered, This word of the Lord came to me...

For the mother of the little boy who died, one of 116 children and 28 adults, when waste from a nearby coalmine slid down the hillside and engulfed a primary school and a number of houses in the village of Aberfan in south Wales on the 21st October, 1966, there never was any meaning, other than the coal board's unpardonable neglect.

On the fortieth anniversary of the event, Christine James captures the dull ache of un-assuaged bereavement in her prize winning poem 'In Expectation', portraying the mother, now in retirement, still waiting and watching for her little boy to come back from school.

As it's afternoon now yet again
like every other afternoon, she yet again
spreads butter thickly on two slices,
sets cheese just so beside the jam
and scalds the tea at three,

an inch of milk poured in a little cup
all ready for him as it always is.

And as it's afternoon now yet again
like every other afternoon, she yet again
goes to the step to scour the street,
combing through fresh faces,
tangled friends,
for a miracle in home-made jumper
running to her as he always would.

And as by now the day is drawing on,
the scrap of tea long curled up on the plate,
she settles, yet again, before the fire,
a weight of wild dreams on her knitting pins;
and knows while watching artificial flame
that nothing now will hinder his return
to her: he comes every night without fail.

For many, therefore, Ezekiel's solution is no solution, but an avoidance of reality. Even so, Ezekiel's search for a meaning that went beyond his own private grief is a deep human instinct indicative of a refusal to accept the meaninglessness of human life.

Around her deeply moving 'Lament for Flora', though still very much alive, Sally Nelson, a former hospice chaplain, nevertheless resists a theology that portrays heaven as a reversal of fortune in which her beautiful and much loved but handicapped daughter, with her 'smile of trapped sunshine' and 'grey green eyes wide to the world', becomes unrecognizably different, forgetting that the resurrected Christ still bears his wounds.

Bound by your chair for years,
there are days when my back screams for mercy,

and my mind is a desert of grief
for all that you are not.

It seems as if, with our best intentions, we find it difficult to conceive of life beyond death as anything other than a simplistic fulfillment of improbable dreams. 'Reversal' and 'spatial' concepts, however, are ultimately totally inadequate to express a dimension of being that is incomparable to anything we currently know. And it may be that science, which was initially held with such suspicion by religion, may prove its unlikeliest ally, because it is the scientists who are questioning whether the basic unit of creation is not a particle but consciousness, or are saying that the universe is information: both of them concepts that also resonate with theological argument.

Between the two extremes of a Heaven, with gold streets and jewelg36 ed gates, and no heaven at all, spirituality encourages the rumor that if God is, then it's not unthinkable (or rather that the alternative is philosophically improbable) that our human journey is just the beginning of a penetration of layers, through and into the very nature of being, and that on the way our characters and our personalities, the 'information' that makes me 'me' and you 'you', will develop and mature. As Nella Last put it, 'somewhere where we get the chances we threw away, or never had, to grow.'

Flip-side

What of Hell, though? Implicit in most theologies of heaven, however conceived, there is, also, a theology of judgment, and judgment implies the existence of 'that other place'! It's not surprising, therefore, that 'as a theological motif', judgment is so problematic for so many Western Christians, as Ian Boxall of Oxford University's Theology Faculty has observed. But what if, as he suggests, we were to see judgment as 'the flip-side of salvation: understood as God's action to put right what is wrong, overcoming injustice'.

Such an approach would liberate us from literal images of a Last Judgment, as represented in the lurid imaginations of those who illustrated the walls of medieval churches, to something much more present, much more immediately disturbing. It would liberate us from conceiving of judgment, not as our lot in some distant, notional, incorporeal existence (which is outside most contemporary Western people's conceptual vocabulary anyway), to see it rather as a very present challenge. It would liberate us to see judgment as a moral wake-up call to our corporate existence in community and in harmony with our total environment.

Judgment, conceived and expressed in these terms, empowers resistance to injustice wherever it exists. It legit-imizes initiatives to overcome oppression and to support those who do. It demands responsibility for the soil as well as the soul.

Judgment, therefore, is not about some settling up of the tally on some supposed day of reckoning in some indeterminate future state, but an immediate response to a present reality. It is what comes between heaven and hell. It is the hell on earth that is the lot of too many, which attracts the attention of judgment. It is about making the kingdom come, in the words of the Lord's Prayer; making it come here and now, 'as it is in heaven'. It is the bringing of salvation to those who are in fear and despair now. It is taking on principalities and powers, 'the great sea monsters', if and as necessary, to restore a quality of life that is everyone's God-given birthright.

It is easy to be distracted or put off by Ezekiel's literal descriptions of the judgment that had befallen his land, with worse to come, as the consequence of a kind of national falling-out with their God. Better and more relevant is to see the connection Ezekiel makes between what has befallen them as a people, and the level of corruption that had become endemic in a society ostensibly dedicated to the one true God. And, as always, with any measured condemnation, it is not the victim who is pilloried, but the powerful, those who:

> ...consume the milk, wear the wool, and slaughter the fat beasts, but you do not feed the sheep. You have not restored the weak, tended the sick, bandaged the injured, recovered the straggler, or searched for the lost; you have driven them with ruthless severity.

Ezekiel remembered the voice of the old prophet, Jeremiah, saying something similar not long before Nebuchadnezzar's invasion: the authorities had abused their position, the people's trust:

> because of them the earth lies parched, the open pastures have dried up. The lives they lead are wicked, and the powers they possessed are misused. For prophet and priest are alike godless.

The priests and the prophets were no less exempt from judgment than those who wielded political power, since it was their special duty to keep the faith, their special responsibility to speak truth to power. No wonder the Bible, with passages like this, has become a textbook for liberationists and, to those in authority, a subversive document!

For Walter Brueggemann, Old Testament professor at Columbia Theological Seminary, a comparison between the approaches of Ezechiel (as he calls him) and Jeremiah can prove quite revealing. 'The issues are much the same for both: they are the only ones we know of who ministered across the discontinuity before and after' the final fall of Jerusalem.

For Brueggemann, however, 'while the issues are the same, their presentations of these issues and their responses to them are different. Ezechiel, unlike Jeremiah, is a priest, and everything is perceived in a priestly idiom. Popular interpretation tends to dismiss Ezechiel as "bizarre". But Ezechiel may be exactly the right text for such a "bizarre" time as ours'.

As Ezekiel wandered along the banks of the Tigris, either alone and deep in thought, or in argument and debate with likeminded deportees, the idea gradually formed in his heart and in his mind that it was one thing to be sure of why calamity had come, it was another to know what that implied for the future, because if judgment was the flipside of salvation, salvation would need to be the flipside of judgment! Where though, was this salvation to be found? And what might it entail?

Dem Dry Bones

Of all the images that have come down to us from this highly spiritual prophet, none is more vivid, more intense, or more memorable than his description of what befell him in a valley littered with the bones of the defeated dead. Had Jeremiah again been midwife to his thoughts? Jeremiah who had forewarned of the same calamity and described the doom of their rulers: the bones of their kings, their high officials, their priests, their prophets, all exhumed and not reburied, scattered across the plain, the carrion to pick at the remaining morsels of decomposing flesh. It was a remorselessly gloomy prognosis.

As Ezekiel contemplated the desert between Babylon and Zion, a different thought took shape in his soul. What if those parched, bleached bones, rather than be left to rot, 'to be dung over the ground', were to be re-animated, to live again, to become the people they had once failed to be?

The Lord's hand was upon me, and he carried me out by his spirit and set me down in a plain that was full of bones. He made me pass among them in every direction. Countless in number and very dry, they covered the plain.

Then he heard the voice of God asking him, 'Can these bones live?' And he answered, 'Only you, Lord God, know that.' And God told him:

Prophesy over these bones; say: Dry bones, hear the word of the Lord. The Lord God says to these bones: I am going to put breath into you, and you will live. I shall fasten sinews on you, clothe you with flesh, cover you with skin, and give you breath, and you will live. Then you will know that I am the Lord.'

Ezekiel seemed to be feeling his way towards an understanding of God that was in advance of his time. Up until then, it had been a relatively simple theological theorem. The people let God down, therefore God lets the people down, and they get carried away into exile: 'as demonstrated'/QED!

Now a new appreciation of what it is to be God began to take shape in his mind. Not a God, like the capricious, unpredictable deities of Babylon, who had to be humored and bribed, but a single, ethical God; a God who does what an ethical God does, not in response to acts of repentance, real or feigned, but because it is what is right.

There is no expectation of confession first, of repentance as a condition. The deportees, either themselves or their children, shall go home, back to Jerusalem. Repentance will be a consequence, not a condition, of forgiveness. His God had grown since his meeting with King Jehoiachin in those early days of exile when he'd pressed for repentance before God would act. There's more in Ezekiel's prophecies that muddy this moment of sublime insight, but let that not detract from acknowledging that in this he was way ahead of his time.

So Ezekiel prophesied as he was bidden, and as he does so, 'there was a rattling sound and the bones all fitted themselves together', captured with memorable simplicity in the traditional spiritual, *Dem dry bones!*:

> The foot bone connected to the leg bone,
> The leg bone connected to the knee bone,

> ... as I watched, sinews appeared upon them, flesh clothed them,

> The knee bone connected to the thigh bone,
> The thigh bone connected to the back bone,

> ... and they were covered with skin,

> The back bone connected to the neck bone,
> The neck bone connected to the head bone,

... but there was no breath in them. Then he said to me, 'Prophesy to the wind, prophesy, O man, and say to it, these are the words of the Lord God: Let winds come from every quarter and breathe into these slain, that they may come to life.' I prophesied as I had been told; breath entered them, and they came to life and rose to their feet, a mighty company.

> Dem bones, dem bones, gonna walk aroun'
> Oh, hear the word of the Lord.

It is a tremendous, thundering climax, and what follows in the remaining record of his prophecies seems banal by comparison. It is as if the orchestra has brought the whole work to a sublime conclusion with a mounting crescendo of drums and a deafening clashing of cymbals, only for the audience to have to sit through the final twenty minutes of something that sounds as if it belongs more to the rehearsal room than to the concert platform!

It is a climax that Ezekiel expects to experience during his lifetime, not in some vague hereafter! We too shall go on missing the point of heaven if we mess up our tenses! It is not about a disconnected, fictional future tense, but a continuity of an already transformed and transforming present. If it is about anything vaguely meaningful, it is about picking up where we will have left off! It will be about a changing that is already underway.

'I shall give you a new heart and put a new spirit within you', Ezekiel hears God saying. 'When will this be? Now?' says Ezekiel. Now. 'I shall remove the heart of stone from your body and give you a heart of flesh'. How? 'I shall put my spirit within you...'

Between the Old 'I' and the New 'I'

Joan Puls, the American Franciscan and one of today's most intuitively practical writers on spirituality, makes this perceptive comment on that passage:

> To be possessed by a spirit is to be consumed, taken over. The spirit of our lives is our total self, who we really are. It is the self that is not confined to time and place. It is the self that spans all our experiences and responses. It is the self that is our truest being. Spirituality is the process that leads to true selfhood.

That process will vary from one faith tradition to another. For the Jews, drawing on the inheritance of Ezekiel, it will be through faithfulness to the law and observance of the distinctive rituals of a chosen people. For the Muslims, it will be by keeping to the Five Pillars of Islam: belief in the Oneness of God, observation of daily prayers, charitable giving, fasting, and, for those who are able, undertaking a pilgrimage to Mecca. For Buddhists, it will be through the discipline and practice of meditation, and by keeping the Five Precepts: not to take a life, not to take what is not given, to practice sexual morality, to refrain from intoxicants, and to adhere to the truth. For Hindus, it will be a long pilgrimage through successive rebirths, determined by constant good living. Sikhs and Jains, Zoroastrians and the Baha'i will also have their own way of expressing how 'dem dry bones gonna walk aroun' again'! While, for the Christian, as Joan Puls expressed it, it will be 'a movement into Christ's great spirit'.

Few have expressed the meaning of that with greater intellectual honesty and conviction, as well as personal integrity, than the German theologian, Dietricht Bonhoeffer. Hanged by the Nazis in the death throes of their iniquitous Reich, the process of achieving true selfhood involved him in a costly engagement with the earthly powers.

In one of his lectures, he described himself with disarming self-awareness, as 'separated from the "I" that I should be by a boundary which I am unable to cross. This boundary,' he explained, 'lies between me and myself, between the old "I" and the new "I". I am judged in my encounter with this boundary.'

It was Bonhoeffer's insistence that our spirituality cannot be separated from our involvement in, and as part of, society that still gives his writings such enduring relevance, and challenges those who see faith as somehow divorced from the reality of everyday life, to think again.

'At this place I cannot stand alone,' he affirmed. 'Here Christ stands, in the center, between me and myself, between the old existence and the new. So Christ is at the same time my own boundary and my rediscovered center, the center lying between "I" and "I" and between "I" and God.'

*

When some of the passersby in Madison Square, New York, in the spring of 2010, chanced to look up, what they saw were numerous figures in various poses dotted around the tops of the skyscrapers. Some called the emergency services, mistaking the fiberglass and iron shapes for potential suicides. Others recognized them for what they were, namely Event Horizon: life- sized installations by the British sculptor, Antony Gormley.

Gormley's art is all about exploring the boundaries between the spaces we occupy, particularly the space within which we exist, namely our own bodies, with many of his sculptures based on his own. So he takes exception to the easy way we speak of 'my body', claiming it is 'a space not a thing, not an object to be improved, idealized or whatever, simply to be dwelt in'. But he is also interested in how one space relates to another space, and the boundaries that define and explain us. In these spaces, that are our bodies, he sees the seeds of who we will be, and the clues to what we have already been, experienced and endured.

Educated at Ampleforth, the Benedictines' premier boarding school in North Yorkshire, Gormley rejected the strict Catholicism of his upbringing in favor of Buddhism. 'Everything I was brought up with was about the fate of my eternal soul, and whether it was going to go to heaven or hell,' which he now believes distanced him from the real, from 'the way things really are, which is that things change from moment to moment and the best we can hope for is to be responsive and responsible, from moment to moment.'

In his art, Gormley is affirming that what we are about as human beings is not where we might go when our bodies are no more, but what we are now, in the bodies that are our primary space.

It is a strangely similar approach to that of Bonhoeffer's, though expressed in different terms, because both reject a view of life which is defined, and lived, solely in terms of some ultimate judgment beyond the grave. Both reject a denial of the reality of the flesh, and both see the point of existence in terms of reconciling the different shapes of who we are, within the spaces that contain and define us. Bonhoeffer's, 'the boundary can only be known as a boundary from beyond the boundary', is, therefore, not such a far cry from Gormley's attempt through sculpture, 'to materialize the place at the other side of appearance where we all live.'

Such thoughts and ideas may seem remotely academic compared with Bella's down to earth admission, 'I don't believe in heaven', or Nella Last's yearning for that 'somewhere where we got the chances we threw away, or never had, to grow'. They are, nevertheless, subtly and securely linked, because they get us away from images that limit rather than release the imagination. They free us from concepts of heaven that are picturesque if improbable, to see it as something which grows out of a journey that we've already started.

They get us away from the hell of medieval imagery, without also losing the idea of judgment, and of the place of judgment in confronting evil and righting wrongs in our journey towards true selfhood. And they open up the prospect of God as one who is not so distant that we cannot also imagine how God can, and does, walk beside us 'in the garden at the time of the evening breeze'.

It is the ultimate in-between, the one that makes all the other in-betweens possible, and love is its name.

Hallowed

7. On Reaching Middle Ground

Let us be like the lines that lead to the center of a circle
Uniting there, and not like parallel lines, which never join
Hasidic saying

As we have chased and dodged the petulant currents, ambled and dawdled over the shambling streams that have coursed through our story between the Jordan and the Tigris, it seems to have exposed a competition of differently paced options, forever vying for the spiritual pilgrim's attention. As we have been drawn at one time this way, at another that way, it is as if the message of the waters is that fulfillment is always to be a matter of avoidance.

In some cases, the choices have been so extreme that they imply that the journey to the infinite sea will be unending, our quest for synthesis and wholeness, for integration and summation, incapable of resolution and best abandoned.

Or if not that, at least that we ought to accept and be content with the interim, harvesting the fruit of spirituality wherever its sprouting shoots edge their defiant way through cracks in the unforgiving soil and jagged fissures in the timeless rock; to acknowledge that the restless quest for a quality and a depth of being is not met in the ping-pong of the either/or: of religion or atheism, of your faith or mine, of magic or mystery, of merciless or merciful, of heaven or hell; to recoil from the extremes that ruthlessly rubbish the alternatives, or that drive the fanatic to impose, when persuasion fails, careless of the pain, the mayhem and the suffering caused by perverted passions.

But is that all that we can expect? Always to be between two rivers, never to experience the coming together when those waterways merge and flow into each other, their excesses diluted, their deficiencies corrected, to tumble carelessly, joyously, singing and foaming together into the broad sea of an infinity teeming with life and energy; the original stuff out of which it was said that all things came to be, and to which all of creation is also believed to be moving.

Is yearning for completeness the forlorn hope of our human lot, nature's cruel little joke, always to travel, never to arrive? Or is it an indication of an impulse built into our genetic information, our DNA, that our spiritual destiny, despite so many indications to the contrary, is nevertheless to achieve that complete harmony with all that is, that was and that shall be; that we are meant to be at one with the source and origin of all life for always, and that on the way, there are numerous opportunities for mending the slits in the fabric of life, healing the hurts, suturing the wounds, bringing together the separated, harmonizing the discords?

So there is one remaining image in Ezekiel that is in stark contrast to all the angst of his previous prophecies. After the wheels and the wings, threatening and terrifying, after the dramatized bondage, after the out-of-body experiences, and the restless, ominous sense of doom and destruction, after the loss of speech and the scroll-eating, after the wound of bereavement and the suppressing of mourning, this final, gentle, satisfying image.

Ezekiel was to take two separate pieces of wood; they may have been the leaves of a writing tablet, or more likely two staves representing the authority of a tribal chief (like the rods or wands entrusted to wardens as badges of office in a parish church today). These would be immediately understood by Ezekiel's contemporaries to refer to the two separated Hebrew kingdoms, the two sovereignties, North and South, Israel and Judah, that may never have been as united as later tradition would claim, but which, in Ezekiel's hands, God had destined to become one.

> This is the word of the Lord to me: 'O man, take one leaf of a wooden tablet and write on it, "Judah, and the Israelites associated with him." Then take another leaf and write on it, "Joseph, the leaf of Ephraim and all the Israelite tribes". Now bring the two together to form one tablet; then they will be a folding tablet in your hand. When your fellow-countrymen ask you to tell them what you mean by this, say to them ... Thus I shall make them one tablet, and they will be one in my hand.'

Implicit in that acted parable was the strong impression that only when those two were one, would Ezekiel's people be able to fulfill their destiny as God's harbingers of a better world.

> In days to come
> the mountain of the Lord's house
> will be set over all other mountains,
> raised high above the hills...

an earlier prophet had proclaimed:

> All the nations will stream towards it,
> and many peoples will go and say,
> 'Let us go up to the mountain of the Lord,
> to the house of the God of Jacob,
> that he may teach us his ways
> and that we may walk in his paths.'

It is this idea of unity, not for its own sake, but because each act of reconciliation contributes to the ultimate well-being of the larger whole, that makes Ezekiel's final prophecy so important and so relevant in a world still stricken by strife.

Here was not some localized ideal affecting a couple of insignificant, inconsequential states that had been all but wiped-off the map of sixth-century BCE geopolitics, compared with the seemingly enduring grandeur of empires like Assyria and Egypt, Babylon and Persia. Here was an outrageously far-sighted discernment that there are some places and some people where, unless they are got right, nothing else will come together as completely and as harmoniously as it should. Such places are like the key moves in solving a Rubik Cube, where the problem remains insoluble unless and until those initial moves are correctly made.

All divisions have the potential to destabilize a much more extensive area than their immediate purview, like oil slicks hundreds of miles out at sea that eventually work their way inland to coat wildlife and habitat in a kind of Black Death. Some divisions, though, have a significance that stabs at the very heart of a world in turmoil, and for historic and continuingly strategic reasons, that place, more than any other, is the city that Ezekiel called Zion.

Between the Jordan and the Tigris there is, therefore, a longstanding fault line that continues to affect and to destabilize the entire world as it draws other interests and other powers into its self-defeating, self-destroying orbit.

'The greatest schism in the people of God and the greatest challenge to the ecumenical movement is division, not between Catholic and Protestant or between East and West,' James Dunn, professor of Divinity at Durham University once challenged the churches of Britain, 'but between Jew and Christian. Only when that is healed will the purpose and promises of God be fulfilled.'

For those for whom Christian schism is a cause of continuing distress, Dunn's words will strike a particularly challenging note, and there is undoubtedly an intrinsic necessity for a coming together of the broken bits of the Christian Cross and the Star of David that will make the world a better place for all. But that will not be enough in itself, unless the Crescent of Islam is not also part of the solution.

According to the old, old story, there were two mothers to two boys: Hagar was Ishmael's mother, Sarah was Isaac's. But they had the same father, Abraham. These are streams that have taken their descendants in disastrously different directions – disastrous for them and disastrous for wider, world harmony. To make a political solution possible there must also be some kind of spiritual transformation in the perception of each about themselves and about the others.

Peace is the reward for those who recognize that preserving the uniqueness or supremacy of their particular faith pales into insignificance before acknowledgement of the one God, the source and goal of all that is, and was, and is to come.

The Growing Gap

Are unity and integration deliberately, intrinsically elusive, or are they more a trick we play in our own minds to avoid an engagement in which we fear we might be disappointed or even rejected?

When the cautious prince, Pwyll, Lord of Dyfed, in a tale in the Medieval Celtic Cycle known as The Mabinogion, saw the headstrong Rhiannon, riding by, like a veritable goddess on her pale-white steed, we are left in no doubt that it was love at first sight. Reluctant to appear too eager, however, and conscious of his status, the prince sent his steward to catch up with her. But the boy on foot was no match for the phantom rider. Returning breathless, he reported that however fast he ran, the greater the gap that opened up between them. So the seed is sown. Here is a prize to be forever wished for, but never to be granted.

Undaunted, the prince then sent one of his companions after the girl, this time on horseback. But again the same thing happened. The faster Rhiannon was pursued, the greater the gap that opened up between them.

Here is a consummate storyteller who not only knows how to spin a tale, but understands what makes his listeners tick in real time. Not only is the object of the prince's quest seemingly unwilling to accommodate herself to her pursuer's intent, but deludes her pursuer into believing in his own mind, whatever the reality on the ground, that the gap between them grows ever wider.

For many, the pursuit of the spiritual seems equally elusive. The more they pursue it, the greater the gap that seems to separate them from the realization of their hopes. The more the urge to bring the two leaves of Ezekiel's vision together, the greater the impossibility of it ever coming true for them. Unity seems to be perversely elusive; God to be unreachable!

When the poet Cowper mislaid his cat, only to find it a couple of days later, stuck in a wardrobe drawer, he blamed the pampered pet for its misfortune, rather than his own inability to find it! 'Beware of too sublime a sense / Of your own worth and consequence', he scolded pompously, whereas the real significance of the incident was much simpler and rather more troubling:

That whatsoever thing is lost,
We seek it, ere it come to light,
In every cranny except the right!

On our spiritual journeys, we expend so much energy and endure so much angst because we are not always looking in the right places. So where is God to be found? How is God to be known? Where is God for us now? Spirituality doesn't set out to provide a definitive answer, but it suggests that we might get nearer to knowing if we were more prepared to live with a creative uncertainty, picking up clues here and there, looking out for signs, testing, rather than rejecting, all the spirits outright.

R. S. Thomas is very much the poet of the searching seeker because he knew what it was to stand in that crossing place between the secular and the sacred, as priest and as poet.

> It is when one is not looking
> ...that it comes.

Thomas may have been as difficult to know as he is to read, but in his bishop he found someone who understood and respected him intellectually and spiritually. In a perceptive monograph on Thomas' 'Poetry of Faith', the bishop explains that Thomas believed organized religion 'had too great a desire to tidy things up', because 'religious belief was essentially precarious and provisional. Too often it wanted to claim too much and often wanted to give answers when there were more questions to face.'

> We have over-furnished
> our faith. Our churches
> are as limousines in the procession
> towards heaven.

Spirituality is essentially untidy. That is its genius. For all his extraordinary visions, Ezekiel never actually gets to see God, only to be shown the warm-up acts!

Similarly, in the Christian scriptures, where Jesus is accorded the title of 'Emmanuel', God with us, recognition is more often a reflection in retrospect rather than in the actual encounter. Even in those insightful moments when a disciple or an enquirer seems to penetrate the mystery face to face, it is only as it was recalled afterwards.

So the Jesus to whom we are introduced in *The Shadow of the Galilean* by Gerd Theissen, onetime New Testament professor in Heidelberg University, is a Jesus who never actually appears, though the narrative keeps pace with his movements from boyhood to manhood. Jesus is only revealed in the effect he has on others. We know him, as Andreas in Theissen's tale got to know him, because his shadow has crossed our path.

If spirituality reminds us that God, more often than not, is experienced indirectly, it also makes us realize that we come upon God by stages, and then never completely in this life. Damascus Road conversions recounted as a flash of blinding light and a voice from beyond may not only be rare, but may actually be false.

There may be something initially enticing in the suggestion made by one Methodist divine to another during some inconsequential nineteenth century theological dispute, that 'the truth doesn't lie in the *via media*, in the middle way, but in both extremes'. It is, however, a false analysis, because it ignores the fundamental problem with all extremists, that they are congenitally incapable of conceding that the opposite may contain any truth worth considering.

Far better, is the approach offered by the Vice Chancellor of one of our oldest universities that, 'The borders separating our societies from each other are blurring...' Spirituality is one such blurring. In a world of religious extremism, its quietly inclusive contribution should not be underestimated in promoting a life of faith that is generous and supportive to those of all faiths and of none, and which promotes values that are of benefit to the debates that take place in the public square. The Quaker poet, Philip Gross, captures the nuances of an inclusivity that is not thrown by difference in these lines from his 'Severn Song':

The Severn was brown and the Severn was blue –
not this-then-that, nor either-or,
no mixture. Two things can be true.

Whatever happened to the New Testament Saul, an Israelite by race, of the tribe of Benjamin, a 'Hebrew born and bred', in his practice of the law 'a Pharisee', and in his zeal for religion, a self-confessed 'persecutor of the church', it happened in the context of prolonged external investigation and internal enquiry. Behind all the apparent certainties with which he went on to articulate his new faith, his subsequent correspondence reveals a mind and a spirit that was in a continuous state of enquiry. Paul's letters are not chapters in a completed work of refined 'dogmatics'; they are a work in progress, and it is that which makes them both fascinating and exasperating!

In that respect, they bear uncanny comparison to the writings of Ezekiel. He bombarded his fellow exiles with messages and images of growing intensity, and was forever unsettling them, particularly his family and friends, with behavior that frequently verged on the extreme. He acted as he did because he refused to be satisfied with facile answers and handed down explanations. We can make a lot or a little about each of those episodes in Ezekiel's life, but their significance lies in their cumulative effect. He repeated the questions endlessly. He pushed his faith to the limit. His was the spirituality of the winding quest.

Jesus' parables similarly emphasize that God's bright new world doesn't come easy. A room needs to be turned upside down to find some missing money; a landowner sends a succession of estate managers to collect revenue misappropriated by corrupt tenants; a diligent farmer has to wait until harvest to see that his efforts have not been wasted.

From John of the Cross to the Mother Julian of Norwich, from Hildegard of Bingen to the twentieth-century CE monk, Thomas Merton, the experience of the spiritual pilgrim has always been a succession of 'dark nights of the soul'.

The life of faith is never tidy, never completed. It is a growing into, with insights accumulating, spasmodically, all too rarely, with long, thick patches of the dense fog of not knowing. It is a walking alongside of the Other, who is both knowable and unknowable, who emerges, momentarily, out of the familiar, during a pub lunch at a wayside inn for a couple of disorientated hikers on their way to Emmaus one Passover week end. Only to flip back to the ordinary as soon as rumbled!

It is a journey towards a knowing that is a self-knowing, which is also about something more, of a need to 'feel the Greatness and the Glory, and all those things that begin with a Capital Letter', in the throwaway line of a fictional character.

In Pursuit of the Elusive Divine

If one difficulty to be overcome in the pursuit of an integration of opposites is the delusion of the elusive, another is often the limitations of those expectations. When the Medieval storyteller introduces a new element into the story of the prince and the rider, it is to tease our curiosity with the suggestion that if it is not the rider who is increasing her speed, then something else must be at work to make it seem that the gap is growing ever wider between them.

Both prophet and Celtic story teller, though they may have lived a millennium and a half apart, were grappling with big issues in uncertain times. Ezekiel's settled sixth-century BCE world had effectively collapsed; his country never to be an independent monarchy again. For the Celts too, invasion and colonization had created reciprocal anxieties.

The society, economy and the church in this Western corner of Britain would be as transfixed and transformed by the Anglo-Norman invasion as Ezekiel's Hebrews had been by the might of Babylon. In both cases, conquest and colonization had brought an end to national independence. What remained, and what ultimately mattered, was a sense of a distinctive identity, an awareness of their roots in a long-remembered past, and a belief (in the words of the most ecumenical of twentieth century Welsh poets, Gwenallt):

...that God had made our nation

For his own purposes

And that its death would be a breach of that order...

All over the world, there are minority ethnicities intent on safeguarding their cultures and traditions, their languages and beliefs, in a context of being subsumed or taken over by more dominant powers, from the indigenous people of North America and Australasia, to the Tibetans in China and the Armenians in Turkey.

The potential of religion in shaping our post-modern society is, therefore, on a knife edge at present. Renewed interest in religion as a serious component in the national and international mix has been fuelled by a confident Islam, whose profile has grown in Europe, largely as a result of immigration.

So the battle-lines between believers and unbelievers are being drawn up more sharply than at any time in our recent history. The assertive atheism with which this third millennium opened, and which thought it had seen off religion as a significant player in the development of a modern, scientific future for humankind, has been made to pause in its tracks. But equally, religion has found itself confused and divided.

We are at a crossroads. And the question that matters, and is likely to decide the shape of Europe and of the whole of the West in the near future, and, by implication, its foreign policy options and decisions, is: What kind of religion? Unless this question is disentangled from the wider religion versus a secular one, both sides in the debate will continue to make false assumptions about each other, to the detriment of universal social cohesion and personal wellbeing.

It would be a mistake, therefore, to assume that the unity of all faiths is the goal to which we should aspire. Rather, we should aspire to a unity of intention and insight between all those who are spiritually aware in all faiths, and those who may call themselves secularists, but whose hearts and minds express all the values that are spiritually precious.

For Ezekiel, it was a matter of probing his people's religious memories to find the God he'd feared they'd lost, while for the Celt it required an unraveling of her people's love of enchantment to expose their spiritual roots. Where was God, Ezekiel persisted? Where was Rhiannon, echoed the Celt: Rhiannon who enshrines mystery, who is both flesh and blood, but also belongs to another realm? For prophet and storyteller alike, the issue is a pursuit of the elusive divine. It remains the central religious issue still.

The Proximity of God

We pick up the story to find that a speedier steed had been summoned from the royal stables, so that the faithful courtier could stand a better chance of catching the girl and bringing her back to his master. 'He came to the open, level plain, and set spurs to the horse, but the more he spurred the horse, the further she drew away from him;' adding, mysteriously, 'She was going at the same pace as when she had started.'

Perhaps it was best to start slowly, trotting and cantering, so as not to frighten the beautiful apparition on her pale-white mount. But when even that proved futile, not surprisingly the pursuing rider gave the hunter its head. And again the same thing happened. Rhiannon's pace seemed constant, but the distance separating them grew ever wider.

We play the same trick in our pursuit of the Divine. We say the God we seek is moving ever further away, back into our childhood, or to some innocent but unlikely past. But what if it is not God who is increasing the distance between us, but we ourselves?

She is not drawing away from him; he is drawing away from her.

It is the limitation of our own hearts and minds that distorts and stretches the distance. We exaggerate the ground to be covered because we are afraid of what the encounter may demand of us. God wants to be found.

Nowhere is the proximity of God expressed in more startling language than in the fiftieth sura of the Holy Qur'an. 'We created man,' says Allah. 'We know what his soul whispers to him: We are closer than his jugular vein.'

When the Celtic horse-goddess was being pursued by the Prince's representatives, they were unable to catch up with her, however fast they ran or rode, though 'she was going at the same pace as when she had started'. It may be a tale of myth and magic, where readers and listeners alike expect its characters to operate in extra-terrestrial ways, but behind the storyteller's art, there is a hint of something more real: something that rooted the fable in a world they knew, of a changed way of life, of dreams unrealized. The distance that separates us from the object of our desire may often belong more to the realm of the mind than of the flesh; that we may imagine the gap to be wider than it is, may even make ourselves believe it, but only because we do not know how to bridge it.

Jerusalem (Zion) may have been countless days' journey from Babylon, but it was not an impossible one. Armies traversed it, exiles were marched across it, traders regularly led their caravans to and fro, across its desert sands and mountain ranges. For Ezekiel, however, and for his fellow exiles, it was an impossible distance, because it was the distance between where he and they now were and where they wanted to be. It was the distance between a newness that felt alien, and a recalled way of life that had been safe. It was the distance between Hamlet's initial uncertainty, whether 'to be or not to be', and his more confident conclusion that, 'There is a divinity that shapes our ends'.

By the rivers of Babylon we sat down and wept
as we remembered Zion.

On the willow trees there
we hung up our lyres,
for there those who had carried us captive
asked us to sing them a song,
our captors called for us to be joyful:
'Sing us one on the songs of Zion.'
How could we sing the Lord's song in a foreign land?

It was the distance between the certainties of the faith they'd grown up with and which had defined their way of life. Zion was where they'd come to know God. And now they were in a place where their God seemed not to be.

It was H.V. Morton, one of the twentieth century's most intrepid travelers, who observed that there was 'a splendid defiance about Jerusalem, or perhaps it would be more correct to say that no people who did not believe themselves to be in the special care of God would ever have built a city in defiance of all the laws of prudence.'

If I forget you, Jerusalem,
may my right hand wither away
let my tongue cling to the roof of my mouth
if I do not remember you,
if I do not set Jerusalem
above my chief joy.

Distance expressed in these terms is more psychological than actual. And it can lead to the most unhappy consequences. We can distance ourselves from people and situations out of pride or prejudice to the extent that the distances become so ingrained that we feel the need to build walls to maintain them: walls we reinforce and extend pathetically as if the real danger was physical rather than the product of our fear to be changed by an encounter with another who might expand our horizons.

Spirituality is wary of all distances.

The Expression of a Need

The final obstacle to be overcome is perhaps the most difficult, because it involves the articulation of our deepest longings.

Throwing all caution to the wind, the thwarted lover in the medieval tale eventually decided to take to the reins himself. 'He turned after her, and let his spirited, prancing horse go at its own pace. And he thought that at the second leap or the third he would catch up with her. But he was no closer to her than before. He urged his horse to go as fast as possible. But he saw it was useless for him to pursue her.'

Even when the Prince took up the chase in person, he was no less frustrated in his quest than all his forerunners, from stable boy to favored courtier. Always, it seemed that, 'the more he spurred the horse, the further she drew away from him', though it is again emphasized that 'she was going at the same pace as when she had started'.

What finally broke the spell? What brought Rhiannon to his arms? What succeeded where all his previous efforts had proved futile?

He talked to her!

In desperation, he called out, 'for the sake of the man who loves you most, wait for me'. And she replied in what must be one of the wittiest, and also one the most underrated lines in ancient literature: 'I will wait gladly, and it would have been better for the horse if you had asked that a while ago!'

Poor horse, she says. Poor man, she means!

The word was made flesh! The prince stopped living inside his head and found the words to address to the girl he sought. He made personal contact. A relationship was established, not because he'd tracked down his quarry like a dumb animal, and cornered her, but because he'd recognized her personhood, her right to receive him or to pass him by.

He could have taken her interest for granted, since she'd repeatedly turned up where he'd notice her. But, equally, he could have doubted her seriousness, assumed that she was no more than a flirt, since all his previous attempts to catch up with her had proved futile. He couldn't know for sure, really know, until he'd risked his princely self-esteem, his fear of rejection and his lack of confidence, concealed by his station and the toys of his position.

It was a big risk to call out to her like that: to articulate his deepest feelings, to say out loud, 'for the sake of the man who loves you most, wait for me'. And when it was done, when the words were out, when the longing had been spoken, there was the silence, as long as the distance between them, waiting for her answer. Would she stop? Would she let him catch up with her at last? Would they ever meet?

And then the relief; the gap closing, the drawing alongside her, and those words he was longing to hear, 'I will wait gladly'; the 'gladly' showing that she wanted him as much as he wanted her. And later the meeting of minds, the clash of intellects with that sublimely unromantic, playful, pointed response, 'and it would have been better for the horse if you had asked that a while ago!'

Ezekiel's longing was to return to Zion; to rebuild, not just the desecrated, dilapidated temple and the razed city walls, but his people's nationhood, Judah, in a restored relationship with the God he'd thought drawing further away from him the more he'd sought to close the gap.

Do not forsake her, and she will watch over you;
love her, and she will safeguard you;
cherish her, and she will lift you high;
if only you embrace her, she will bring you to honor.

But Judah, too, had a longing: a longing to be united with Joseph, her northern neighbor. Perhaps they'd never been one unified state, one original Israel, and the exploits and grandeur of Saul, David and Solomon had been more wishful thinking than historical fact. In Ezekiel's heart, though, they belonged together, Judah and Joseph: two small countries, buttressed and buffeted by vast empires to the north, to the south, to the east, Assyria, Egypt, Babylon, Persia. They shared a common tongue, they refrained from similar food, but pre-eminently, they had the same distinctive, if imperfect, understanding of the Divine.

So there comes a point at which we too need to gather up our thoughts, and speak the prayers, express the longing, light the candle, cross the threshold, be 'hallowed', made holy, conse-crated, if we are to find our 'hearts of stone' replaced, as Ezekiel prayed, with 'hearts of flesh'. It is the articulation of all the secret longings, of all the un-dared-for hopes, of all the missing needs of our incomplete selves. It is a recognition of the good in many of the spiritualities we might otherwise have dismissively thought of as 'godless'.

Then the rivers, that both enticed and repelled us at different times, may finally find their resolution as they sink together into the swell of the vast ocean beyond. The gentle Ystwyth that trickles its way down from the high Pumlumon range, and the terrier Rheidol, bounding and bouncing with confident eagerness to get to the sea, finally coming together in a bay that frees them from all the constraints, inhibitions and bravado of their long journey homewards.

The Tigris and the Jordan may not meet in so obvious a way, but they too eventually find their resolution in the waters beyond; the one to the saltiest sea on earth, the other to the Gulf below Iran.

It is a consummation that is a parable of the spirituality that bridges every difference of conviction. It is a realization of all that it means to be human. It is taking the wheat and the yeast and losing both in the bread that sustains and satisfies. It is the fire that bakes and the water that binds. It is seeing God in others. It is the audacity honestly to see oneself as the very image of the Divine. It is the hallowing, the consecrating, the dedicating to God, of the ordinary.

> Let us be like the lines that lead to the center of a circle
> Uniting there, and not like parallel lines, which never join.

*

As they wend their way home along the church-peppered, chapel-salted streets in the town between two rivers, what do they think? What do they see? As they make similar journeys in all the other towns and hamlets, conurbations and cities, from Belfast to Beijing, from Denver to Delhi, what do they hope for? What do they expect? No less than those on the long road back from Babylon to Jerusalem; that 'this most tremendous tale of all' might still retain its power to change them, and the world, for good.

Acknowledgements

Ezekiel as the inspiration for exploring contemporary spirituality was prompted by a passing reference in a wonderful little book on 'everyday holiness' by the American Franciscan, Joan Puls (*Seek Treasures in Small Fields*, DLT, 1993).

Ezekiel also takes me back to a question I was set in my finals, on the significance of his emphasis on individual responsibility. I have little recollection of how I answered it at the time, other than that it seemed to satisfy the examiners! Since then, I have come to appreciate more of the significance of Ezekiel as one of the architects of an evolving faith.

Along the way, many people have broadened and deepened my spiritual awareness, and helped, wittingly and otherwise, to bring this book to completion, among them:

Heather Cobby, who discussed the work of the Anglo-Welsh poet, Edward Thomas, with me; Cytûn for photocopying facilities, supervised by Sasha Periam, my supportive PA when I was General Secretary; Marc Dummer, for sermons that twinkle with humor and learning; Ellen, my daughter, for teaching me to savor Shakespeare; Peter Francis for inter-faith hosting at Gladstone's Library; Emyr Humphreys for permission to quote from his poem, 'The Serpent'; Toby Field for efforts to trace a long forgotten radio program; Ted Hale for his pioneering of a neglected George Matteson hymn; Bridget Hewitt for her 'Pondering the Mystery' reflections in the Living Spirituality Network newsletter; Jennifer Galvin for proofreading the typescript; John Garland for insights into Tolkien; Richard Griffiths for invaluable advice on tracing sources; Philip Gross for permission to quote from his 'Severn Song'; my publisher, John Hunt, and his production team, for again pulling off the miracle of translating a manuscript into a finished book; Stuart Jackson, my friend from our days as fledgling ministers in

Coventry, who told me about Nella Last; Christine James for permission to use 'In Expectation'; Dave Legumi for memories of 'Mosaic'; Iain McQueen, whose persistent questioning of all things spiritual I have never been able to satisfy, but whose conversation and company has never failed to stimulate; The Merton Legacy Trust for permission to quote from Merton's translation of 'The Ascent of Mount Carmel' by St John of the Cross; Abdalla Yassin Mohamed, for encouragement in dialogue; John Morgans for drawing my attention to the relevance of a Brian Wren hymn; Robin Morrison for his intuitive inter-faith poem; Neill Murdoch for improving my cosmology; Sally Nelson for permission to quote from her poem 'Lament for Flora'; Owain, my son, for scientific know-how, and back cover photo; Anthony Thacker for conversations on the *via media*; Gwynno Thomas for permission to quote his father R.S. Thomas; Sr Vincent, who introduced me to the writings of John O'Donnohue; Hilary Wakeman for tracking down a poem in her SHOp poetry magazine; and John Watt, for letting me borrow his signed copy of Finkelstein and Silberman.

Much appreciation is also owing to those willing to risk their reputations by offering endorsements in advance!

I owe a particular debt to Angela Graham, who offered creative suggestions and constructive advice on the manuscript and the title, and helped clarify what I had unwittingly obscured!

Most of all, my greatest debt is to Denise, my wife, whose thoughts and insights over the years have influenced me far more than she realizes, and whose questions and comments on reading an early draft, when it was barely more than an indistinct scan in a pregnant womb, set me on the road to making lots of improvements.

None, however, can be held responsible for any shortcomings in the final version, which remains solely mine.

Every attempt has been made to acknowledge sources, and if

any have been inadvertently missed, my sincerest apologies, and assurance to redress omissions in any reprint.

Sources

Extracts from the Book of Ezekiel and other books of the Bible, unless stated otherwise, are from the Revised English Bible version (OUP 1989).

Where I have drawn on Good as New: A Radical Retelling of the Scriptures (o-books 2004), these passages have been marked in the Biblical References below.

The phrases, above the chapter heading, are from the opening verses of the book of Genesis in Albert Pietersma and Benjamin G. Wright's New English Translation of the Septuagint (Oxford 2007).

Background

Some of the sources I've found particularly useful:

Karen Armstrong: The Great Transformation (Atlantic books 2006)

Walter Brueggemann: An Introduction to the Old Testament (WJK 2003)

Keith W Carley: The Book of the Prophet Ezekiel (CUP 1974)

Israel Finkelstein & Neil Asher Silberman: The Bible Unearthed (Free Press, Simon & Schuster 2001)

J Galambush: Ezekiel, in John Barton & John Muddiman, ed: The Oxford Bible Commentary (OUP 2001)

Fleming James: Personalities of the Old Testament (Scibner 1963)

H W F Saggs: The Greatness that was Babylon (Sidgwick & Jackson 1962)

Frontispiece

Bridgett Hewitt: 'Pondering the Mystery' in Living Spirituality News (Summer 2009)

Ezekiel 37: 9 & 10

Walter Brueggemann: Hopeful Imagination (Fortress Press 1986)

Stanley Hauerwas: Hannah's Child: A Theologian's Memoir (scm press 2010)

1. Making for the Middle Ground

Shakespeare: Hamlet (III, i, 55)

John Betjeman: Christmas in Collected Poems (John Murray 1958)

James Shapiro: 1599: a year in the life of William Shakespeare (faber and faber 2005)

Lesslie Newbigin: The other side of 1984 (WCC 1983)

Robert Runcie in a Sunday Times review of Ann Wroe's Pilate: the Biography of an Invented Man (Vintage 2000)

Jocelyn Bell Burnell: Television interview, Beautiful Minds (BBC4 April 2010)

Harry Eyres, The Slow Lane column in the Financial Times 2009

Rheidol and Ystwyth: Niall Griffiths: Real Aberystwyth (Seren 2008)

Biblical References (in order):
Ezekiel: 17: v 9
Psalm 22: v 2
Psalm 22: v 11
Jeremiah 8: v 8
Ezekiel 3: v 3
Psalm 19: vs 9a & 10

2. Between Religion and Atheism

Gerald Manley Hopkins: God's Grandeur (various anthologies and online)

Philip Pullman: interview with Amanda Mitchison (Financial Times 3/4 April 2010)

Vaclav Havel: interview with Stephen Wagstyl (Financial Times 5/6 July 2008)

Edward Thomas, Light and Twilight (Kessinger Publishing 1911)

Owen Martell: *Cadw dy ffydd, brawd* (Gomer 2000). Author's translation.

Charles Darwin: Gillian Beer's introduction to the Oxford World Classics edition of On the Origin of Species (OUP 2008)

Aled Jones Williams: *yn hon bu afon unwaith* (bwthyn 2008). Author's translation.

Martin Buber: I and Thou (T & T Clark 1966)

Khalil Gibran: The Cedars of Lebanon (various anthologies and online)

Shakespeare: Henry V (III.i.1, 15-17)

Simon Phipps: God on Monday (Hodder and Stoughton 1966)

God of the gaps: 'the phrase is generally derogatory, and is inherently a direct criticism of a tendency to postulate acts of God to explain phenomena for which science has yet to give a satisfactory account.'

Biblical References (in order):
Ezekiel 7: v 26
Ezekiel 33: v 21
Job 2: v 9
Ezekiel 16: vs 39b, 40b, 41a
Ezekiel 36: vs 24, 25, 26, 27
Ezekiel: 18: v 2
Revelation 3: vs 15 & 16
Ezekiel 10: vs 18a, 19a, & Ezekiel 11: v 23

3. Between Your Faith and Mine

George Matheson: Gather us in (older hymn books)

Leigh Hunt: Abou Ben Adhem and the Angel (various anthologies and on line)

Samuel Huntingdon: The Clash of Civilizations (Touchstone 1998)

Rowan Williams: Writing in the Dust (Hodder & Stoughton 2002)

Khalil Gibran: The Prophet (various anthologies and online)

S. Wesley Ariarajah: Not Without My Neighbour (WCC 1999)

Dalai Lama: *Agence France-Presse* 9 Oct 2006

Focolare: 'an international organization that promotes the ideals of unity and universal brotherhood. Founded in 1943 in Trento, northern Italy by Chiara Lubich as a religious movement, the Focolare Movement, though primarily Roman Catholic, now has strong links to the major Christian denominations and other religions, or in some cases, with the non-religious.'

Perry Schmidt-Leukel and Lloyd Ridgeon: Islam and Inter-Faith Relations (The Gerald Weisfeld Lectures 2006)

When I fall to my knees: in Let us break bread together, American spiritual (various hymn books)

Mark Tully: Lives of Jesus (BBC Books 1996)

The lightening strike of the cross: Robin Morrison (robinmorrison@churchinwales.org.uk)

Biblical References (in order):
Ezekiel 8: vs 1-3a
Ezekiel 8: v 3b
Genesis 8:v 22
Ezekiel 8: v 16

4. Between Magic and Mystery

St John of The Cross: The Ascent of Mount Carmel, stanzas 3&4, Thomas Merton's

translation in The New Man (Burn & Oates 1962)

Charles Wesley: And can it be that I should gain (in many hymn books)

Merton: a biography by Monica Furlong (1985 DLT)

Rumi: cited in Annemarie Schimmel: The triumphal Sun (Albany 1993), quoted in

Schmidt-Leukel and Ridgeon: Islam and Inter-Faith Relations (above)

Christopher Partridge: The Re-Enchantment of the West, volumes 1 & 2 (T & T Clark 2005)

Euan Cameron: Enchanted Europe: Superstition, Reason and Religion 1250-1750 (OUP 2010)

David Albert Jones: Angels: a History (OUP 2010)

Woman in the crowd: Verena Wright: Maid in God's Image (DTL 2008)

Hellenistic magic: Eric Franklin in the Oxford Bible Commentary (2001), quoting J.M. Hull:

Helenistic Magic and the Synoptic Tradition (SCM 1974)

Gregory Collins: Come and Receive Light (Columba 2003)

John O'Donohue: *anam cara*: spiritual wisdom from the Celtic world (Bantam 1997)

Moltmann: stmellitus.org/resources

Diarmid O'Murchu: Ancestral Grace: Meeting God in our Human Story (Orbis 2008)

Diarmaid MacCulloch: A History of Christianity (Allen Lane 2009)

Women, Church and Society in Wales, ed. by Gethin Abraham-Williams (Cytûn 2004)

Emyr Humphreys: The Serpent, adapted from Gwenallt's *Y Sarff*, in Collected Poems (Cardiff University Press 1999)

Flora Winfield: in Kathy Keay's Dancing on Mountains (Harper Collins 1996)

on *eucatastrophe*: see http://www.tolkien-online.com/on-fairy-stories.html

The Penrhys Festival: Angela Graham: Culture and Occulture – an alternative to

scandalous religion? in: The Furrow, a journal for the contemporary church (2009)

John Morgans' account of Penrhys in Journey of a Lifetime (2008 from jonomo@btinternet.com)

For the Society of Penrhys: www.ourladyofpenrhys.co.uk

Biblical References (in order):

Acts 8: v 9 and following: Good as New (o-books 2004)

Ezekiel 43: vs 1-3

I Samuel 28: v 7 and following;

Exodus 22: v 18

Luke 8: v 42b and following: Good as New (o-books 2004)

Leviticus 15: v 25 and following

Ezekiel 10: vs 6, 13, 16a, 19

Genesis 1: v 27

Genesis 2: v 22

Judges 5: v 7

5. Between Merciful and Merciless

Brian Wren hymn: Great God, your love has called us here (Rejoice & Sing, OUP & URC 1991)

John Milton: Samson Agonistes, lines 33-35, various anthologies and online

Shakespeare: The Merchant of Venice IV. i. 187-190, various editions and online

Margaret Atwood: Payback (Bloomsbury 2008)

Forgiveness in: Faith without Reason, by Herbert McCabe (continuum, 2007)

The Dominicans are a religious order in the Catholic Church specifically devoted to preaching and study, hence their being sometimes called Friars Preachers. During the middle ages they supplied many of the leaders of European thought (with Thomas Aquinas one of their number). Traditionally champions of learning and orthodoxy, it is as such that they are still today one of the most influential of the religious orders.

The Prince of Wales: The Dimbleby Lecture 2009

(http://www.princeofwales.gov.uk)

Karen Armstrong: The Case for God: What Religion Really Means (Bodley Head 2009)

Imagined endearments are based on sayings from the Biblical Song of Songs

Scapegoat: Concise Oxford English Dictionary definition.

Chiara Lubich: The Cry (New City 2001)

Biblical References (in order):

Matthew 5: v 7

Mark 14: v 36

Ezekiel 16: vs 7a, 8, 13b, 14a

Matthew 18: v 22 Good as New (o-books 2004)

Galatians 5: vs 14b & 15 Good as New (o-books 2004)

Levitics 16: vs 21 & 22

Psalm: 22: v 1

Ezekiel 33: v 7

6. Between Heaven and Hell

Christine James, her own translation of her original Welsh poem, first published in The SHOp poetry magazine, issue 25

Nella Last's Peace, ed Patricia & Robert Malcolmson (Profile Books 2008)

TV Film: Housewife, 49 (2006)

Gregory the Great, attributed with remarking on the fair-haired British children he saw reduced to slavery in Rome: *Non Angli sed Angeli, si forent Christiani (Not Angles, but Angels. If they were to be Christians...)*

Mary Lee: In Between: PiF Magazine (February 2004)

http://www.pifmagazine.com/2004/02/in-between/

Sally Nelson: The Whitley Lecture 2009, A Thousand Crucifixions (Regent's Park College, Oxford)

Vlatko Vedral: Decoding Reality: The Universe as Quantum Information (OUP 2010)

Amit Goswami's theory that consciousness is what causes matter to come into being is much more controversial, e.g. God is not dead: what Quantum Physics tells us about our origins and how we should live (Hampton Roads Publishing 2008)

Ian Boxall: The Books of the New Testament (SCM 2007)

Walter Brueggemann: Hopeful Imagination (Fortress Press 1986)

Joan Puls: Seek Treasures in Small Fields (DLT 1993)

Keith Clements: The SPCK Introduction to Bonhoeffer (SPCK 2010)

Antony Gormley interviewed by Aida Edemariam (The Guardian 22 May 2010)

Biblical References (in order):
Matthew 6: vs 9b – 13 / Luke 11: vs 2b – 4
2 Corinthians 12: v 2 Good as New (o-books 2004)
Ezekiel 24: v 18
Ezekiel 24: vs 16b & 17
Ezekiel 24: v 19
Ezekiel 34: vs 3 & 4
Jeremiah 23: vs 10 & 11a
Jeremiah 8: v 2
Ezekiel 37: vs 1 & 2
Ezekiel 37: vs 4 – 10
Ezekiel 36: vs 26 & 27

7. On Reaching Middle Ground

Hasidic Saying: Robert E Tornberg: The Jewish Educational Handbook (Behrman House 1998)

Sioned Davies: The Mabinogion, a new translation (Oxford 2007)

William Cowper: The Retired Cat (1791), various anthologies and online,

e.g. http://www.luminarium.org/eightlit/cowper/cat.htm

Methodist Divines: Charles Simeon, a friend of John Wesley, in relation to the theological debate over free will or predestination. Reference: courtesy of Rev. Robin Wood, Methodist Minister, South Wales District.

R S Thomas: when one is not looking, in Collected Poems 1945-1990 (Phoenix 1990)

R S Thomas: over furnished our faith, in Counterpoint (Bloodaxe 1990)

Barry Morgan: Strangely Orthodox (Gomer 2006)

Andrew Hamilton, vice-Chancellor, University of Oxford, in a promotion letter, July 2010

Philip Gross: The Water Table (Bloodaxe 2009)

Gwenallt: Dewi Sant, various anthologies including: Seasons of Glory (1997 Cytûn)

Qur'an: sura 50: 15, and following, a new translation by M. A. S. Abdel Haleem (Oxford 2004)

For religious restructuring, see various articles by James L Guth, Furman University (http://ps.furman.edu/faculty/nelsen/publications.html)

H.V. Morton: In the Steps of the Master (Perseus Books 2002)

Biblical References (in order):
Ezekiel 37: vs 15–19
Isaiah: vs 2 & 3
I John: 4 v 1
Psalm 137: vs 1-6
Proverbs 4: vs 6-8

Also by Gethin Abraham-Williams

Spirituality or Religion? Do we have to choose?
(O-books)

SIMON BARROW, Co-Director Ekklesia
Reconnects rhetoric with reality

Rev Dr TONY CAMPOLO, Eastern University, Pennsylvania
Not only has it good things to say, but is brilliantly written

Rev Dr KEITH CLEMENTS, former General Secretary
Conference of European Churches
Touches a real contemporary nerve

Rev Dr DAVID COFFEY OBE, President, Baptist World Alliance
A generous and adventurous book

MARTIN CONWAY, former President, Selly Oak Colleges,
Birmingham
Explores the spiritual dimension in an illuminating way

Rev Dr DAVID CORNICK, General Secretary, Churches
Together in England
*This wise, generous and humane book cannot fail to enrich and
enlarge our understanding of the ways of God with human beings*

Rev Dr ROBERT ELLIS, Principal, Regent's Park College,
Oxford
*Packed with insights that will encourage those tempted to give up on
religion*

JOHN HENSON, New Testament translator
Has an important message for the 21st century

Eley McAINSH, Director, Living Spirituality Network
A challenging and provocative book

Rt Rev CLEDAN MEARS, formerly Bishop of Bangor
Compelling and refreshing

Most Rev Dr BARRY MORGAN, Archbishop of Wales
A book that will stretch our minds and imaginations and also move our hearts

Sr JOAN PULS OSF, former Superior General, Sisters of St Francis, USA
I recommend this thought-provoking book to anyone who is a disciple and a seeker

Rev JOHN RACKLEY, former President Baptist Union of Great Britain
Written in a lyrical style that beguiles what it explores, there is a sharpness of analysis beneath the surface that is not satisfied with easy answers

MIKE STARKEY, Church Times
Wisely retorts that 'religion' and 'spirituality' as popularly used are simplistic and unhelpful

MARK TULLY, Presenter Something Understood, BBC Radio 4
Featured in the 'To Change or Not to Change' broadcast

HILARY WAKEMAN, Editor, Open Spirituality N/L (Ireland)
Wrestles creatively with the question in its title

Circle Books

Circle is a symbol of infinity and unity. It's part of a growing list of imprints, including o-books.net and zero-books.net.

Circle Books aims to publish books in Christian spirituality that are fresh, accessible, and stimulating.

Our books are available in all good English language bookstores worldwide. If you can't find the book on the shelves, then ask your bookstore to order it for you, quoting the ISBN and title. Or, you can order online—all major online retail sites carry our titles.

To see our list of titles, please view www.Circle-Books.com, growing by 80 titles per year.

Authors can learn more about our proposal process by going to our website and clicking on Your Company > Submissions.

We define Christian spirituality as the relationship between the self and its sense of the transcendent or sacred, which issues in literary and artistic expression, community, social activism, and practices. A wide range of disciplines within the field of religious studies can be called upon, including history, narrative studies, philosophy, theology, sociology, and psychology. Interfaith in approach, Circle Books fosters creative dialogue with non-Christian traditions.

And tune into MySpiritRadio.com for our book review radio show, hosted by June-Elleni Laine, where you can listen to authors discussing their books.

MySpiritRadio